W9-CXN-684

The Wreckers' Tower Game

based on Enid Blyton's
Five go down to the Sea

Illustrated by Gary Rees

HODDER AND STOUGHTON
LONDON SYDNEY AUCKLAND TORONTO

British Library Cataloguing in Publication Data ·

The wreckers' tower game.
  1. Games—Juvenile literature
  2. Adventure and adventurers—Juvenile
literature
  I. Blyton, Enid
  893.9   GV1218.A3

  ISBN 0-340-35871-8

First published 1984
Second impression 1985

Published by Hodder and Stoughton Children's Books,
a division of Hodder and Stoughton Ltd,
Mill Road, Dunton Green, Sevenoaks, Kent TN13 2YJ

Printed and bound in Great Britain by
Hazell Watson & Viney Limited,
Member of the BPCC Group,
Aylesbury, Bucks

You have often read about The Famous Five's adventures . . . now here's your chance to take part in one!

This time YOU are in charge. YOU have to work out the clues, read the maps, crack the codes. Whether The Five solve the mystery or not is in your hands.

You will not necessarily solve the mystery on your first attempt. It may well take several goes. Keep trying, though, and you will eventually be successful.

Even when you *have* solved the mystery, the game can still be played again. For there are many different routes to the solution – and each route involves different clues and adventures.

So the game can be played over and over. As many times as you like!

HOW TO PLAY

To solve the mystery, you have to go with The Five on an adventure through the book. You do this by starting at PARAGRAPH ONE and then following the instructions to other paragraphs.

Many of the paragraphs will ask you to work out some sort of clue. You do not have to work out every one of the clues to solve the final mystery . . . but the more you manage, the more you're likely to be successful. The less clues you crack, the less chance of completing the adventure.

To help you work out the clues, there are several pieces of equipment available - a torch, a measure, a map and a codebook. You can start with only *one* of these EQUIPMENT CARDS but you will often pick up others as the game goes along. Occasionally, however, you will be asked to give some up as well.

To hold your EQUIPMENT CARDS during the adventure, there is a RUCKSACK CARD. This will tell you exactly which EQUIPMENT CARDS you have for use at any one time. Any EQUIPMENT CARDS not in your rucksack **cannot be used or consulted** - and therefore should be kept out of play.

Of course, no Famous Five adventure could take place without provisions. You are therefore given three PICNIC CARDS. These are to be kept in the slit of the LUNCHBOX CARD.

Every time The Five eat or lose some of their provisions, you must remove one of the PICNIC CARDS from the LUNCHBOX CARD. When there are no PICNIC CARDS left in your LUNCHBOX, your provisions have run out and so you cannot possibly continue with the adventure. The game is over and you will have to start again from the beginning.

READY TO START

The Famous Five are JULIAN (the biggest and eldest), DICK, GEORGE (real name Georgina, but she always wanted to be a boy), ANNE and George's dog, TIMMY.

They have gone to Cornwall for their holidays, where they are staying at Tremannon Farm with the farmer and his wife, Mr and Mrs Penruthlan. The farm is in an isolated spot and not far away is the wild, deserted Cornish coast.

They have not been there long before they become bothered by a rather grubby little boy. His name is Jan and he insists on following them wherever they go. Timmy seems to have taken quite a liking to him but the rest of The Five just find him a bit of a nuisance.

One day Jan takes The Five to see his grandad, an old shepherd who lives on the hills. Demonstrating with his pipe, the shepherd tells them how the nearby coast used to be the haunt of *wreckers*. They would flash a false light from a tower to lure ships on to the rocks. They would then go and plunder the wreckage.

This was a long time ago, but the tower - known as The Wreckers' Tower - still exists. It is now a ruin, hidden somewhere in a dip in the cliffs. The Five are fascinated by the story and they become even more fascinated when the shepherd tells them that, on some stormy nights, the tower still flashes!

Could it be haunted? Or is the old shepherd just imagining things?

The Five decide to go in search of the ruined tower ...

To join them on this search, you will first of all need to put on your rucksack. So pick out the RUCKSACK CARD and have it near to you. You must now choose *one* piece of equipment to take with you. Which do you think would be the most useful – a torch, a measure, a map or a codebook? Insert the EQUIPMENT CARD you have chosen into the slit of your RUCKSACK CARD and keep the remaining three EQUIPMENT CARDS out of play until told you can pick them up.

Now for your provisions. Mrs Penruthlan has kindly prepared The Five a delicious picnic of sandwiches, cherry cake and ginger beer. Put the three PICNIC CARDS into the slit of your LUNCH-BOX CARD. Don't forget to remove a PICNIC CARD every time The Five are instructed to eat or lose some of their provisions.

Remember: When there are no PICNIC CARDS left in your LUNCHBOX, the adventure has to stop and you must start all over again.

Good luck!

1

Having said goodbye to the farmer and his wife, The Five set out through the farm gates full of excitement. They walked briskly, Timmy wagging his tail in front. 'I knew it wouldn't be long before we found ourselves on another adventure,' Julian said happily. Of course, they did not tell the farmer and his wife where they were going. The grown-ups might not like the idea and they thought it best to keep it secret. Anyway, it might well be that they could not find The Wreckers' Tower. Only very few people in the area had even heard of it – let alone were able to tell where it was! Before long, The Five came to a country lane but it soon branched several ways. 'Which way do we choose?' asked Dick, scratching his head. They all suggested a different way and even Timmy seemed to have a preference of his own!

To decide which of The Famous Five to follow, throw the special FAMOUS FIVE DICE. If you throw mystery, you must take that route instead.

JULIAN thrown	go to 211
DICK thrown	go to 284
GEORGE thrown	go to 51
ANNE thrown	go to 181
TIMMY thrown	go to 235
MYSTERY thrown	go to 256

2

'Well, I don't see any footpath,' said Dick when they had reached their ninetieth and last pace. But, as they looked around them, they suddenly noticed a short section of track cut into the slope above. This was the only spot from which any of the track could be seen. They hurried in its direction. ***Go to 245.***

3

'What's going on?' yelled the man as he was suddenly dazzled by the bright beam. A second later and Timmy had jumped at him, snarling at his wrist. 'Well done, Timmy!' they all shouted as they made their escape. They kept running along the tunnel, only coming to a stop when they were sure the men were well behind. 'What a pity they all had masks on so we couldn't see who they were,' said Julian. Then they noticed Timmy had something in his mouth. Not only had he made the man drop the gun but he had also taken a codebook from him!

If you don't already have it, put the CODEBOOK CARD into your RUCKSACK. Go next to 175.

4

They followed George up the narrow, crumbling steps. She examined each step carefully before treading on it to make sure it was safe. On one of the steps she found a message chiselled into the stone. 'What does it say?' the others asked eagerly from behind. 'I'm afraid it's in code,' she replied. 'Does anyone have a codebook ready?'

Use your CODEBOOK CARD to decode the message. If you don't have one, go to 72 instead.

LpJG

5

Entering the police station door, they were surprised to see The Barnies there. The Barnies told them that their Guvnor had gone missing and they had come to report it. But The Five couldn't talk for long because they were anxious to tell the sergeant about the gang. As soon as the sergeant had heard their story, he summoned together all his men. They hurriedly accompanied them back towards the farm but on the way the sergeant's torch went out. The Five quickly searched through their rucksacks to see if they had one that still worked.

*Use your TORCH CARD to light up the rest of the way by placing **exactly** over the shape below. If you don't have one, go to 102 instead.*

```
(/GINH:,   ONMBHU  FR  ?MKJ:TIJHG  I OF
   VJ?E  HBNI     BUGG! HMN      T D!JM:
   MNB        GFRYG FDERG       ?&BJG
 MN  SLKFT   I:LOU!   UYR!  I!SK:(AS X)
```

6

'Here it is!' cried George, finding a narrow hole in the rock. They quickly crawled in, hearing the men's voices right behind. 'I wonder where this tunnel leads?' asked Dick as they hurried along. It seemed to go on and on but they kept going, knowing that they daren't turn back. The men might well have come into the tunnel as well! Then they heard a voice echo from a long way back. Yes, the men had come in! 'Oh, do hurry, Timmy,' scolded George when he suddenly stopped, 'this is no time to be picking up bones!' But then she realised that it wasn't a bone he had picked up at all – but a torch!

If you don't already have it, put the TORCH CARD into your RUCKSACK. Now go to 175.

Anne stepped over the threshold, the rest right behind. The inside was very dusty and full of old rubbish. Many of the floorboards had rotted and they had to be careful where they trod. Dick suddenly noticed a message carved into one of them! Unfortunately, it was in code.

Use your CODEBOOK CARD to decode the message — then follow the instruction. If you don't have one, go to 237 instead.

LpDRgF

'It's a good job there's a full moon,' said Anne as they continued to climb, 'or we wouldn't see a thing.' She noticed a large cloud moving across the sky, however. She only hoped they reached the top in time! *Go to 249.*

They all followed Dick out of the farm gate and on to a small country road. He must have made a mistake, though, because the police station wasn't in the direction he thought. They were just wondering which way to go next when they noticed a parson coming along on his bicycle. 'Excuse me, sir,' said Dick, running up to him, 'but can you tell me the way to the police station? It's rather important.' The parson scratched his head for a moment. 'Well, let me see,' he hummed. 'Yes ... you take the turning 80 metres back down this road.' No sooner had the parson left them than they quickly searched their rucksacks for a measure.

Use your MEASURE CARD to measure the 80 metres — then follow the instruction there. If you don't have one, you'll have to guess which instruction to follow.

Go to 62

Go to 188

Go to 38

10

Anne's idea was to take a little footpath that branched off to the left. 'I bet this circles round to the back of the cliffs,' she said, 'and then leads up.' To begin with, it looked as if she was right. The path grew steeper and steeper. But instead of the clifftops all they reached was an old windmill! They were well and truly lost. 'No need to despair!' said Julian cheerfully, having an idea, 'we can look up the windmill on the map. Then we'll soon find the right way.'

Use your MAP CARD to find out which square the windmill is in – then follow the instruction. If you don't have one, you'll have to guess which instruction to follow.

If you think C3	go to 212
If you think B3	go to 100
If you think D2	go to 135

11

'Yes, there it is – over there!' they all said at once as they suddenly glimpsed the sea. They could see a tiny strip of blue in the gap between the two distant ridges. Take one step backward or forward, though, and it suddenly disappeared! Heading for the gap, they came across a shepherd's hut. It looked as if it had been abandoned long ago but then Julian suddenly thought he heard a noise from inside. There was another surprise. Just about to enter, they found a crumpled-up map wedged into the window frame. Since it didn't seem to belong to anyone, they decided to take it.

If you don't already have it, put the MAP CARD into your RUCKSACK. Now go to 45.

12

'He probably meant us to go this way,' said Julian, once they were on their own again. He led them through a field of sheep and towards a signpost in the distance. The signpost did indeed point to the sea – but it pointed in the direction they had just come! Before they walked all the way back again, Anne suggested having some of their picnic to refresh themselves.

Take a PICNIC CARD from your LUNCHBOX. Now go to 110.

13

'So that means this wall must be facing west,' said Julian when they had found the windmill. They all looked round for Anne. She had suddenly disappeared! 'Here I am,' she said, straightening up, 'I've just found this on the floor.' It was something round and made of rubber. They put it up to the hole for a better look. 'It's a torch!' exclaimed Julian. 'Well done, Anne – that's exactly what we wanted.' The room became a lot brighter with the torch and they noticed a trail of cigarette ash on the floor. 'Then someone *has* been here recently!' said Julian with excitement as they started to follow it.

If you don't already have it, put the TORCH CARD into your RUCKSACK. Now go to 187.

14

'Well, not much further now,' said Julian. 'I can't wait until we see that beautiful blue sea.' They couldn't wait until they saw the tower either. Did it really still flash on some nights? It certainly was a mystery. So curious about it were they that they ran all the way down the next hill!

Run with them to 95

George was right! *POLICE STATION – $\frac{1}{4}$ MILE* read the sign pointing west. 'It's lucky we had a torch,' said Anne as they hurried in that direction. They were lucky to have a torch for another reason. They had only gone a little way further when its beam lit up a codebook on the ground! 'That might be useful,' said Julian as they entered the police station gate.

If you don't already have it, put the CODEBOOK CARD into your RUCKSACK. Now go to 35.

'We'll just have to guess which is the correct branch,' said George when they found the message wasn't any help. They decided on the one that went to the right. But after quite a bit more walking they came to a dead end. They had some of their cake on the way as they returned to the other branch.

Take one PICNIC CARD from your LUNCHBOX. Now go to 178.

Suddenly, the wind dropped for a while and the flag was impossible to read. They were sure it must be flying from the tower however. So they decided to head in its direction and investigate. Before they started, though, they agreed to have a little of their picnic. They might well need the energy for whatever adventures might lie ahead!

Take one PICNIC CARD from your LUNCHBOX. Now continue to 70. (Remember: when there are no picnic cards left in your lunchbox, you must start the game again.)

18

The coded message said that the goods would be arriving on the Friday night. 'That's today!' they all exclaimed with a thrill. But they wondered what the goods were and why there was such secrecy about them. They had only gone a few metres further when they discovered something else on the ground! It was a torch. They took it with them, thinking that it might well be useful if theirs ran down.

If you don't already have one, put the TORCH CARD into your RUCKSACK. Now go to 40.

19

Julian's suggestion didn't find the path again but it did take them past an old tree stump. Carved into the stump was a coded message! 'I bet it says how much further to the way out,' said Julian excitedly as they all looked through their rucksacks for their code-books.

Use your CODEBOOK CARD to decode this message. Then follow the instruction. If you don't have a CODE-BOOK CARD in your RUCKSACK, go to 84 instead.

20

Anne offered the policemen some of her sandwiches on the way. 'Thanks very much, miss,' one of them replied. 'We had to leave the station just before our tea!' On tasting Mrs Penruthlan's sandwiches, however, they declared that they were glad that they had!

Take one PICNIC CARD from your LUNCHBOX. Now go to 86. (Remember: when there are no picnic cards left in your lunchbox, the game is over and you must start again.)

21

Using the torch to light up the ground in front, they slowly continued. George's torch suddenly caught something white in the grass. Picking it up, they realised that it was a map! 'This could be handy,' said Julian, putting it in his rucksack. The storm had now cleared and they were able to proceed much faster to the top.

If you don't already have it, put the MAP CARD into your RUCKSACK. Now go to 152.

They suddenly saw something move further up the path. They wondered what it was but then they realised it was just a rabbit. Timmy bounded after it before they could stop him. 'Oh, do be careful!' shouted George. 'You don't know how safe the path is.' But it was too late! The next thing they heard was a loud crash followed by a long whine. They dashed up the path after him, eventually finding where it had given way. Then they heard Timmy's whine again. 'It sounds as if he's fallen on to a ledge just below,' said Julian. But it had become so dark that they would need a torch to help rescue him.

Use your TORCH CARD to light up the ledge by placing exactly over the shape below – then follow the instruction. If you don't have one, go to 258 instead.

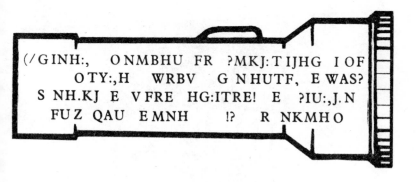

Anne soon wished that she hadn't chosen the way after all. She had brought them to a wide river and there appeared no way of getting across. 'We always seem to have this trouble!' laughed Dick. Suddenly, Timmy vanished. The next time they saw him he was standing on the opposite bank! 'He must have swum,' said Anne. 'No, he couldn't have,' said George, 'look – he's perfectly dry!' Then Timmy showed them how he had done it, leading them to some stepping stones a little further along. 'Oh, isn't this fun!' exclaimed Dick as they balanced from one stone to another. 'More than fun,' replied Julian with an idea, 'it might also show us where we are on the map.'

Use your MAP CARD to find out which square the stepping stones are in – then follow the instruction. If you don't have a MAP in your RUCKSACK, you'll have to guess which instruction to follow.

If you think C1	go to 200
If you think A3	go to 280
If you think A2	go to 71

Dick led them down towards an old lighthouse. It stood just out to sea, perched on a battered rock. 'This isn't the way to the clifftop!' laughed Julian. But then Dick told them his idea. They could use the lighthouse to find out where they were on the map. Then they could see if there were any footpaths nearby leading up to the cliffs.

Use your MAP CARD to find out which square the light-house is in – then follow the instruction. If you don't have one, you'll have to guess which instruction to follow.

If you think B4	go to 83
If you think A4	go to 114
If you think B3	go to 162

25

It led to another coded message a little further up. Again, they had to use their codebook. This one told them that they were exactly half way up. ***Go to 290.***

26

They were about to set off when Anne found something in the road. It was a measure! 'It must have dropped off The Barnies' wagon,' said Dick, 'let's see if we can catch them up and return it.' They ran as fast as they could but it was no use – The Barnies were well out of sight. 'We'll just have to give it back at their show,' said Julian as they returned. Then they thought The Barnies probably wouldn't mind if they borrowed it for a while. It might well come in useful as a spare!

If you don't already have it, put the MEASURE CARD into your RUCKSACK. Then go to 110.

They kept walking through the wood until finally they reached a field. At the far end of the field was an old farmhouse. It looked as if it had been deserted a long time ago but then Julian thought he saw a light go on and off inside. 'Let's go and ask them if they know the way,' he said. Just as they reached the farmhouse, Dick suddenly realised something. He had lost his torch! He must have left it on the ground when they helped Timmy dig up that tin.

If you have one, remove the TORCH CARD from your RUCKSACK. Now go to 45.

They all held on to the back of each other's jackets, ready to start walking. 'This way no one will get lost,' said Julian. ***Go to 163.***

The tunnel was very dark but with the help of their torches they finally reached the other end. 'I wonder how they managed to get their barges through?' asked Dick. 'There's hardly room to put a paddle.' They all looked towards Julian for an answer. He always knew the answer to things. 'Quite simple,' he replied, 'the bargemen would lie on their backs and tread along the tunnel roof.' They all discussed how tiring it must have been as they continued on their journey. ***Go to 158.***

They could climb no further, having reached the very top! They could see for miles and miles below. Not too far away they spotted a flagpost poking out from behind a ridge. From it there flew a large red flag and on the flag there was some writing. 'Do you think it's the tower?' they all asked excitedly. There seemed only one way to find out – to try and read the writing. But when the flag next blew in their direction they saw that it was in some sort of code.

Use your CODEBOOK CARD to find out what the message said by decoding the instruction below. If you don't have one, go to 17 instead.

Suddenly, they spotted a figure down below. He was coming towards the tower! 'Quick, let's go down again and find some-where to hide,' said Julian in a panic. They hurriedly descended the steps and returned to the house part of the tower. Timmy led them to an old fireplace, starting to sniff around it. 'We haven't got time to play any games,' George scolded him. But then Julian noticed that the back of the fireplace looked rather false. He knocked on it. It was hollow! 'Perhaps this is a secret passage,' he said as they began to push at the false back. Sure enough, the back gave way and there appeared a long tunnel right in front of them! They hurriedly crawled in, hearing the stranger now come up to the front door. They were in such a hurry, in fact, that Dick dropped some of his sandwiches.

Take one PICNIC CARD from your LUNCHBOX. Now go to 295. (Remember: when there are no picnic cards left in your lunchbox, you must start the game again).

32

Soon after leaving the pond, they had the impression that someone was following them. Every time they looked round, however, whoever it was had gone. They therefore decided to play a trick on them. The next time The Five disappeared behind a tall hedge, instead of continuing to walk, they would stop right where they were! 'Ssh!' George told Timmy as they waited for the mysterious person to appear. *Go to 275.*

33

'It's so dark in here I can hardly see,' said Julian as he led them in. All the windows were boarded up and the only light came from the half-opened door. 'Do you think we should leave well alone?' Dick asked nervously as the floorboards creaked under their feet. 'No, we've never given up on an adventure before,' Julian replied, trying to be brave. He suddenly trod on something slippery. He bent down to see what it was. It was a patch of oil – still wet! 'That means that someone has been here very recently,' he said breathlessly, 'the oil must have dripped from a lamp.' He then found another patch, then another. 'Let's see where the oil leads,' he suggested, 'I bet it's to the tower part.' But the task would be quite impossible without a torch and so they felt through their rucksacks for them.

Use your TORCH CARD to find out where the oil leads by placing exactly over the shape below. If you don't have one, go to 276 instead.

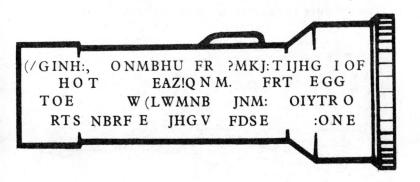

They were unable to find the church on the map, however. They daren't spend any more time looking in case those men came into the tunnel after them. When they had walked a lot further along the tunnel, they decided they were probably safe and could have a quick picnic. Jan's eyes lit up at the sight of the large slice of cake Julian was offering.

Take one PICNIC CARD from your LUNCHBOX. Then continue to 67.

Hurrying up to the sergeant's desk, they were surprised to see The Barnies there. The Barnies said that their Guv'nor had gone missing and they had come to report it. But The Five couldn't talk for long because they were anxious to tell the sergeant about the smuggling gang. When he heard their story, the sergeant immediately called together all his men. The Five started directing them back towards the farm but then they suddenly lost their way. Fortunately, there was one of Mr Penruthlan's signs nearby. *FOR FRESH FARM CREAM* it read, *TAKE TURNING TO LEFT 60 METRES AHEAD.*

Use your MEASURE CARD to measure this 60 metres — then follow the instruction there. If you don't have one, you'll have to guess which instruction to follow.

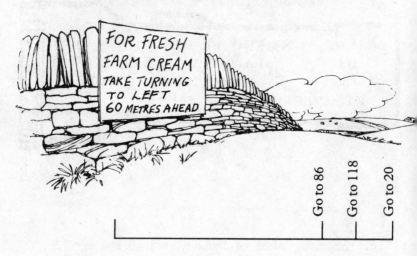

Go to 86   Go to 118   Go to 20

36

In searching for a torch, Julian had emptied his rucksack on to a nearby ledge. As he was putting the things away again, he accidentally dropped his measuring tape. It started to roll along the passage! They all chased after it but the passage sloped so much that it disappeared into the distance. Even Timmy couldn't catch it!

If you have one, take the MEASURE CARD from your RUCKSACK. Now go to 40.

'We're The Barnies,' one of the men on the wagon called down to Julian, 'come and see our show.' They threw him a leaflet which read: *THE BARNIES ARE COMING – WE DANCE, WE SING, WE MAKE YOU LAUGH.* Julian carefully put it in his pocket, promising they would all be there at their next performance. He then asked if they knew the way to the sea. 'Certainly, young master,' the man replied, 'head for the ruined castle. From there it's only the throw of a stone.' Before he could ask where the ruined castle was, however, they had gone. They would have to look it up on their maps instead.

Use your MAP CARD to find out which square the ruined castle is in – then follow the instruction. If you don't have one, you'll have to guess which instruction to follow.

If you think A2	go to 171
If you think C3	go to 50
If you think A3	go to 26

They went right past the turning on their first search but eventually they found it. They decided to eat some of their sandwiches on the way to make it easier to run. All this excitement had made them quite hungry anyway! Just as Dick was finishing his last bite, he spotted the police station ahead.

Take one PICNIC CARD from your LUNCHBOX. Now go to 55.

Timmy sniffed through the hole, the rest squeezing through right behind. They hadn't gone far before the path divided. They were just wondering which branch to take when Anne noticed a coded message chalked on to the tunnel wall. 'I bet it gives the right direction!' said Julian as they searched through their rucksacks for a codebook.

Use your CODEBOOK CARD to decode this message. If you don't have one, go to 16 instead.

L p D R g P

The passage finally came out at a small cove at the bottom of the cliffs. It had grown quite late now and the sky was beginning to go dark. A wave swept right up to within a metre of their feet. The next one came even closer. 'Oh no!' exclaimed Dick, 'the tide's coming in! We had better move quickly.' But they weren't sure where to go. They didn't want to walk all the way along the passage again and the cliffs looked far too steep to climb. 'What are we going to do?' they all asked, rather nervously. Then Jan tugged on Julian's arm. 'Jan know,' he said, 'Grandfather often tell stories of The Wreckers' Way. It's a secret path cut into the cliffs.' So they quickly searched for where the path began. Just as the water started to lap at their shoes, they found it. It was at the far end of the cove, hidden behind a large rock.

Throw the FAMOUS FIVE DICE to decide who is to go up the path first.

JULIAN thrown	go to 230
DICK thrown	go to 101
GEORGE thrown	go to 56
ANNE thrown	go to 97
TIMMY thrown	go to 69
MYSTERY thrown	go to 22

Suddenly, though, the man broke free! The policemen tried to stop him but he pointed a gun at them. He set off across the fields and disappeared into the night. 'Well at least we've caught the rest of the gang,' said the sergeant, 'we'll just have to catch their leader next time. He's sure to try this smuggling business again.' And when he did, thought The Five, they would be there to help foil him!

Your adventure wasn't quite successful. If you would like another attempt at solving the mystery, you must start again at paragraph one.

42

Back came a series of flashes from across the water! The idea had worked! The fisherman's wife told them what the flashes meant and pointed them in the right direction. ***Go to 245.***

43

'What a shame our torches weren't strong enough,' Anne sighed, 'I wonder what the message said?' They also wondered who could have written it. 'Perhaps it told of a secret way to the tower,' said Julian, 'and was written by one of the wreckers!' After all, why else would someone have gone to all that trouble to carve inside a tree!

Continue to 158.

Part way along the dark passage, they noticed a small wooden door set into the rock. Anne pushed it open and stepped through, the rest following right behind. They had entered a large underground cavern! There was a lamp on the floor and Julian lit it with some matches he found, slowly moving it round. The place was full of old chests and crates. They went to examine one of them. There was some writing on the lid but the lamp wasn't bright enough to make it readable. They hurriedly searched through their rucksacks for a torch.

*Use your **TORCH CARD** to make the writing clearer by placing exactly over the shape below ... then follow the instruction. If you don't have one, go to 198 instead.*

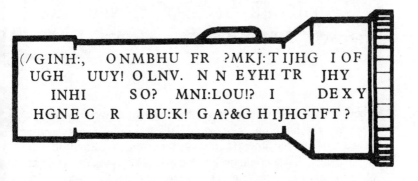

(/G INH:,   O NMBHU FR ?MKJ:T IJHG I OF
UGH   UUY! O LNV. N N E YHI TR   JHY
    INHI   S O?   MNI:LOU!? I   DE X Y
HGNE C   R   I BU:K! G A?&G H IJHGTFT ?

'Ooh, it's awfully dark in here,' said George when they had gone through the rickety old door. Even Timmy seemed to be rather doubtful about it - and he wasn't scared by anything! 'Well, there's nobody here,' remarked Julian after they'd had a good look round,

'I must have imagined it.' Just before they left, though, Anne noticed some sort of inscription in the roof. *FOR A SHORT CUT TO THE WRECKERS' TOWER* ... it began – but the rest was too dark to read. They would need to shine a torch up there!

Use your TORCH CARD to light up the rest of the inscription by placing exactly over the shape below. If you don't have one, go to 174 instead.

```
(/GINH:,   ONMBHU  FR  ?MKJ:TIJHG  I OF
BNJT TUBH   (JBM  WU    GFN:/! O KKF
  INMBHF  OMKJ:MNBGFR  GUNK GJ(R
  AS TH. GJ:H  HB   R LK. ! E ERG     E
```

46

Then Dick suddenly had another idea which would save the batteries for later on. They could use one of their measures instead! At first the others thought he had gone a bit crazy but then he explained. They could use the measure like a piece of rope and all hang on to it. So as long as the person at the front could feel his way, they all could. The idea worked brilliantly. But then they realised they were pulling on the tape so hard that they had stretched it. It was now no good for measuring!

If you have one, take the MEASURE CARD from your RUCKSACK. Now go to 290.

47

This route didn't take them back to their original footpath but it did eventually lead out of the wood. Ahead, there was a small

babbling river. Julian remembered Mr Penruthlan saying that one of the rivers nearby flowed right into the sea. They therefore decided to follow it, hoping this would be the one. 'Once we've found the sea,' said Julian, leading the way, 'we'll soon find the tower.' It was not long before they met a problem, however. The river divided two ways! 'Never mind,' said Dick cheerfully, 'it will at least make it easy for us to find on the map.'

Use your MAP CARD to find out in which square the river divides – then follow the instruction. If you don't have a MAP in your RUCKSACK, you'll have to guess which instruction to follow.

If you think D2	go to 216
If you think B2	go to 296
If you think D1	go to 250

48

When they still couldn't spot the tower, however, they decided to have some of their picnic while they considered what to do next. They found a nice patch of grass nearby. Timmy suddenly gave a strange bark as he was eating a cheese and pickle sandwich. 'What's wrong?' asked George, 'cheese and pickle always used to be your favourite.' They they realised that that wasn't why he was barking at all. His paw was pointing to the top of an old building showing behind a nearby ridge. Had he found the tower, they all wondered excitedly as they ran towards it.

Take one PICNIC CARD from your LUNCHBOX. Then go to 70. (Remember: when there are no picnic cards left in your lunchbox, you must start the game again.)

Suddenly, there was a loud bang from behind! Someone had shut the door on them. They tried to open it but it had obviously been locked as well! 'That'll teach you to come meddling,' said a sinister voice from the other side. They began to shout out but the stranger had gone. Just as they were starting to worry, George noticed a scrap of paper on the ground. There was some writing on it! *JIM – SPARE KEY IS EXACTLY 30 METRES FROM RUM BARREL* it said. Having found the barrel, they started to look for their measures.

Use your *MEASURE CARD* to measure the 30 metres – then follow the instruction there. If you don't have one, you'll have to guess which instruction to follow.

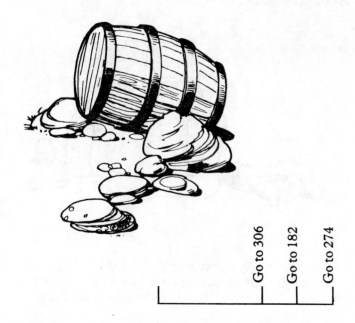

Go to 306

Go to 182

Go to 274

50

They hadn't gone much further before Timmy sniffed out an old bone. 'Well, if you're going to have your picnic,' laughed Dick, 'we might as well have *ours*! You're not the only one who's hungry, you know!' So they all stopped for some sandwiches and some of that delicious ginger beer.

Take one of your PICNIC CARDS from the LUNCH-BOX. Now go to 267.

51

So it was eventually agreed they should follow George's choice. The path led to a tiny village, where there was only one shop! After buying some ice cream from him they asked the kindly shopkeeper if he knew the way to the coast. He told them to take the path along the side of the village pond, only 130 paces from there.

Use your MEASURE CARD to count the 130 paces from the shop — then follow the instruction there. If you don't have a MEASURE CARD in your RUCKSACK, you'll have to guess which instruction to follow.

Go to 161

Go to 151

Go to 89

Suddenly, they heard a noise from below! Someone was trying to push through the door. They decided to rush back to the room at the bottom and find somewhere to hide. Just as they reached the last step, however, Julian noticed a large ring in the stair wall. He gave it a pull. Miraculously, part of the wall opened. It seemed to be some sort of secret passage! They hurried inside as they heard the person come nearer. 'Oh no!' said Dick once the wall had closed behind them, 'I've dropped some cake on the other side. Now they'll know where we are!' Moments later, they saw the wall begin to open again . . .

Take one PICNIC CARD from your LUNCHBOX. Now go to 295. (Remember: when there are no picnic cards left in your lunchbox, you must start the game again.)

53

The path took them way up above the sea. It rose and fell and rose again until the highest point of the clifftops was finally in sight. *Go to 30.*

54

They hadn't walked far along the path before they saw a large piece of paper blowing towards them. It had been whisked up into the air by a sudden wind. The paper dropped on to a nearby hedge. 'It looks like a map,' said Julian, trying to reach it across the branches. Edging a bit closer, he saw that it was indeed a map! 'This could be very useful,' he said, being careful not to tear it.

If you don't already have one, put the MAP CARD into your RUCKSACK. Now go to 95.

They piled through the police station door, surprised to see that The Barnies were there. Their Guv'nor had gone missing and they had come to report it. 'Well, what can I do for you, children?' asked the red-cheeked sergeant at the desk. The Five told him about the gang and how they had trapped them in the farmer's shed. The sergeant instantly called together all his men, asking where the farm was. Julian replied that it was near the water mill and they all looked for a map in their rucksacks to show him.

Use your MAP CARD to find out which square the water mill is in – then follow the instruction. If you don't have one, you'll have to guess which instruction to follow.

If you think A2	go to 20
If you think B2	go to 118
If you think A1	go to 86

George led the way up the steep, rocky path. They were about half way up when the path suddenly divided. They weren't sure which branch to choose. Then Jan noticed some writing painted on to the rock. Unfortunately, it was in code! They hurriedly looked for a codebook, hoping that the message would give the right direction.

*Use your **CODEBOOK CARD** to decode this message — then follow the instruction. If you don't have one, go to 145 instead.*

LpDRgJD

57

Since they couldn't find a torch quickly, they decided that Timmy had better go first. He could see a lot better than the others and he also had a very clever nose! To encourage him, they gave him a large slice of cake. 'There will be another one when you get us safely to the top!' George said, patting him on the head. Timmy wagged his tail, leading the way.

*Take one **PICNIC CARD** from your **LUNCHBOX**. Now go to 249.*

'We can read it!' they all shouted with delight as their torches lit up the hollow. The message told them of a short cut to the local church and from there they would be able to see the coast. When they arrived at the church, they found that it was true! In the distance, there was a bright blue sea crashing against the rocks. There was another surprise. Timmy found an old measure nestling in the long grass! They decided to take it with them.

If you don't already have it, put the MEASURE CARD into your RUCKSACK. Now go to 126.

By the time they had found their torches, however, the crab had disappeared. 'We'll just have to feel our way along the passage wall,' said Dick. The passage became more and more damp and so they realised it couldn't be much further now. Suddenly, George slipped and pulled the others over with her. The contents of their rucksacks spilled all over the rocky floor! They picked them up again before continuing. It was so dark, however, that they didn't notice that they had left a codebook.

If you have one, take the CODEBOOK CARD from your RUCKSACK. Now go to 80.

'We'll just have to try and find our way without one,' said Julian when they couldn't find one that still worked. Fortunately, however, it wasn't long before the moon reappeared and they soon spotted a small stone building ahead. There was a blue lamp on the side, telling them that it was a police station! They hurried towards it, Julian deliberately dropping some of his sandwiches for the birds so that he could run more quickly.

Take one PICNIC CARD from your LUNCHBOX. Now go to 55.

61

As hard as they peered, there wasn't so much as a wave to be seen! 'The sea must be very hidden indeed,' said Dick. They therefore decided to give up the search and climbed down the hill to a small church at the bottom. 'Perhaps the parson will be able to help us,' said Julian. But on reaching the church they found that there was no one around. 'He must be visiting his parish,' said George. ***Go to 126.***

62

The turning led eventually into the nearby village. 'Which building do you reckon is the police station?' asked Julian, anxious not to lose any more time. Then they saw an elderly policeman emerge from one of the doors, ready to start his beat. They decided it must be that one. ***Go to 35.***

Jan was looking faint from all the walking and so Anne suggested stopping for a bite to eat. 'But say those men come into the tunnel?' remarked Dick anxiously. They therefore decided that it would have to be a very brief stop.

Take one PICNIC CARD from your LUNCHBOX. Now go to 67.

64

The code confirmed that the stones were indeed part of an old footpath to the clifftop. 'They must have been laid by farmers long ago,' said Julian. *Continue following this path to 152.*

65

'Look, it belongs to someone called Jim!' Julian said, reading the engraved letters. He put the watch in his pocket as evidence before they continued on their way. *Go to 40.*

Following the signpost's direction, they soon spotted a small stone building ahead. As they came nearer, they saw that there were several reward notices on the wall. 'This must be it!' exclaimed George, hurrying through the gate. *Go to 5.*

They suddenly heard a rough-sounding voice from behind. 'Who's there?' it asked. 'Reveal yourself or I'll shoot!' The next thing they knew, a light was being directed at them and they could hear a gun being loaded. They were just thinking that they would have to give themselves up when George had an idea. They could suddenly shine a torch into the man's face to confuse him while Timmy leapt for the gun. Very, very quietly, they felt for one in their rucksacks.

*Use your **TORCH CARD** to try out this trick by placing exactly over the shape below ... then follow the instruction. If you don't have one, go to 209 instead.*

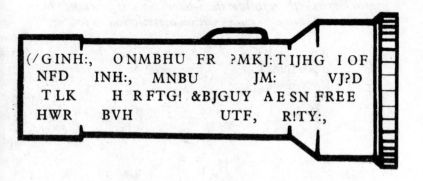

Since they didn't have a torch that still worked, they just had to guess the direction. 'I hope this is the right guess,' said Julian as they hurried along, 'or those men will have time to escape.' Fortunately, it was! It wasn't long before they could see the blue lamp of the police station ahead. *Go to 35.*

Timmy sniffed his way up the cliff, the rest right behind. 'What's that?' asked Anne, pointing to an isolated column of rock just out to sea. 'It's called a sea-stack,' answered Julian. He explained that it was where part of the cliff had become separated by the sea. Then he had an idea. There was a good chance the sea-stack would be shown on the map. It would be a clue to where The Wreckers' Way was, should they want to tell the police. So they searched through their rucksacks to see if they had a map with them.

Use your MAP CARD to find out which square the sea-stack is in — then follow the instruction. If you don't have one, you'll have to guess which instruction to follow.

If you think E3	go to 177
If you think C4	go to 240
If you think D4	go to 207

Yes, they were right! Suddenly, there the tower was – hidden in a dip of the cliffs! Although it was very difficult to see from the land, it would have been quite easy from certain parts of the sea. They again thought of those poor ships being tricked on to the rocks by its flashing light. But they tried to put it out of their minds as they walked right up to the ruin. The bottom part was just like an ordinary house. The tower part was attached to one end and was about twice as high as the house's roof. Cautiously, they went round to the building's front door. It was very stiff and overgrown with weeds but they finally managed to push it open.

Throw the FAMOUS FIVE DICE to decide who is to enter the tower first.

JULIAN thrown	go to 33
DICK thrown	go to 252
GEORGE thrown	go to 169
ANNE thrown	go to 7
TIMMY thrown	go to 255
MYSTERY thrown	go to 93

Dick said it would waste too much time, however, and so they all decided just to guess the way from there. 'Let's try this direction,' said Julian, leading them through a gate towards an old pony track. ***Go to 220.***

They continued to climb, going very carefully so they didn't slip. 'Oh, I'm sure we don't have to go this slowly,' said Dick after a while, becoming more careless. On the very next step, however, he tripped and dropped his bottle of ginger beer. They heard it roll and crash all the way to the bottom!

Take one PICNIC CARD from your LUNCHBOX. Now go to 290.

73

The path seemed to go on and on and it really was quite tiring! 'Let's stop for some picnic,' suggested Anne. With the marvellous view and fresh sea air, it seemed such a lovely place for a picnic that they all agreed.

Take one PICNIC CARD from your LUNCHBOX. Now go to 312. (Remember: when there are no picnic cards left in your lunchbox you must start the game again.)

74

They all followed behind as Timmy put his nose to the ground, sniffing out the way they had come. Suddenly, he stopped! 'What's the matter, Timmy?' asked George, 'what have you found?' Timmy scooped up the soft earth with his paw. 'Why, it's an old tobacco tin!' exclaimed Anne, 'and look – there's a message inside!' When they tried to read the message, however, they found that it was in a secret code.

Use your CODEBOOK CARD to find out what the message said by decoding the instruction below. If you don't have one, go to 27 instead.

L p D R g Y C

75

Part way along the dark passage, they noticed a wooden door set into the rock. 'That's odd to find a door down here!' remarked Julian. They decided to walk through, arriving at a large cavern on the other side! 'It seems to be some sort of storage room,' said Dick, noticing all the old chests and crates. They went to examine some of them. Most were empty but inside one they found a small bible. Opening it up, they saw that it wasn't a bible at all – but a secret codebook!

If you don't already have it, put the CODEBOOK CARD into your RUCKSACK. Now go to 49.

They all followed Dick to a small sheep track he had seen. 'I bet this climbs right to the cliff top,' he said. On the way up, however, the track often went dangerously close to the edge and Anne became a little scared. She was worried that it might become even worse. Then Julian suddenly had an idea! He would go on ahead and make sure it was safe for them. If it was, he would let them know by sending back flashes of his torch.

Use your TORCH CARD to flash out the way to the top by placing exactly over the shape below. If you don't have one, go to 141 instead.

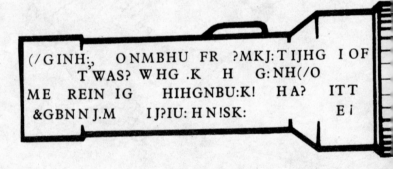

```
(/GINH:,   ONMBHU  FR  ?MKJ:TIJHG  I OF
        T WAS?  WHG .K   H   G:NH(/O
ME   REIN IG    HIHGNBU:K!   HA?    ITT
&GBNN J.M    IJ?IU: H N!SK:           E i
```

'First of all, though,' Julian added more cheerfully, 'how about some of our picnic?' The others eagerly agreed, quite hungry after their little goose chase. 'Well, you don't really deserve any,' said George when Timmy tried to take a bite of her sandwich, 'but I suppose you didn't mean it.' The others were ready to forgive Timmy too. After all, he had always been a lot more of a help than a nuisance on their adventures!

Take one of your PICNIC CARDS from the LUNCH-BOX. Then continue to 275.

78

On their way, Dick tripped on one of the many brambles that clung to the building's walls. His map fell out of his rucksack as he did so. He tried to pick it up but it caught on some sharp thorns and tore into shreds.

If you have one, take the MAP CARD from your RUCKSACK. Now go to 192.

79

Before they went back down again, they decided to have some of their picnic. It was silly to carry all that weight about. And they'd never had a picnic on top of a tower before! 'How exciting!' they all agreed.

Take one PICNIC CARD from your LUNCHBOX. Now go to 92.

80

The passage finally came out at a small cove at the bottom of the
cliffs. They must have been in the passage quite some time
because it had now grown fairly dark. They soon realised there
was another problem. The tide was coming in! 'Another five
minutes,' remarked Julian anxiously, 'and the whole place will
probably be under water.' They wondered what to do. They didn't
want to go all the way down the passage again and the cliffs looked
far too steep to climb. Then Anne noticed a small path cut into the
cliffs' side. 'This must be The Wreckers' Way,' said Dick as they
started to climb. 'Don't you remember Jan's grandfather talking
about it?' Yes, they did – it was a secret path used by the gangs to
escape after plundering the wreckage. *Go to 308.*

81

Timmy made them follow him to a small footpath that ran across
the fields. It soon joined a crossroads. At the side of the crossroads
was a signpost but it was so dark that it was impossible to read. 'I
expect one of these signs points to the police station,' said George
as they felt through their rucksacks for a torch.

*Use your TORCH CARD to find out which way to go by
placing exactly over the shape below. If you don't have
one, go to 68 instead.*

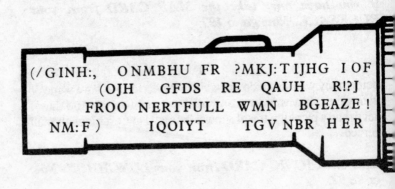

```
(/GINH:,   ONMBHU FR ?MKJ:TIJHG I OF
        (OJH  GFDS  RE  QAUH   R!?J
      FROO NERTFULL WMN   BGEAZE !
NM:F )    IQOIYT    TGV NBR HER
```

'That's better!' said Dick as the torch lit up a good fifty yards ahead. He felt a lot safer now. They continued to climb, hoping that Mr and Mrs Penruthlan wouldn't be too worried about them. They certainly hadn't intended to be out this late! Suddenly, George noticed something white on a ledge a few feet below. 'Oh, do be careful!' said Anne as Dick tried to reach it. He finally managed to grab one corner, bringing it up to have a closer look. It was a map. Not only might it be useful to them but it proved that someone else had been using this path recently!

If you don't already have it, put the MAP CARD into your RUCKSACK. Now go to 249.

They weren't far from the top when George suddenly realised something. She had lost her codebook! It must have fallen out when they were searching for their maps. There wasn't time to go all the way back again and so they decided they would just have to leave it.

If you have one, take the CODEBOOK CARD from your RUCKSACK. Now go to 312.

They finally emerged from the wood into a field. In the middle of the field was a small wooden tower for observing birds. Julian thought he saw someone move inside. 'Let's go and ask him if he knows the way,' he said. They approached very quietly so as not to disturb the birds. *Go to 45.*

A lot further along the passage, George noticed a neatly-folded piece of paper wedged into a crack in the rocky wall. There was a scribbled note inside! It said that the goods were to be buried in one of the islands in the river until all the fuss had blown over. 'I wonder what goods it's talking about?' asked Dick. Julian didn't know but he was sure there must be something illegal about it. He therefore suggested they look up the islands on the map in case they wanted to investigate later on.

*Use your **MAP CARD** to find out which square the river islands are in – then follow the instruction. If you don't have one, you'll have to guess which instruction to follow. follow.*

If you think E2	go to 210
If you think D2	go to 270
If you think B2	go to 225

'Did you get a good look at these men?' the sergeant asked as they hurried through the farm gate. But Julian replied that they had all been masked. 'Never mind,' said the sergeant on entering the shed, 'we'll soon find out who they are now!' He added that they had been after the gang for years and there was a big reward at stake. He ordered his men to surround the trapdoor while he removed the sacks from it. Anne quickly fetched Mr Penruthlan to come and help. They all tensely waited for the men to appear. Finally, the leader of the gang emerged and as soon as he set foot on the ground he was arrested! The sergeant started to pull the mask off his face . . .

Use your CODEBOOK CARD to find out who it was by decoding the answer below. If you don't have one, go to 41 instead.

Xhfo
KqufB
bT

Then Anne had a better idea, thinking their torches might startle it. They could feed the pigeon with some of their cake. The sound of his eating might attract other pigeons and they could listen where they were coming from. It worked! No sooner had the pigeon found the crumbs they threw than others started to arrive. They seemed to be coming from the next room. The Five felt their way towards it.

Take one PICNIC CARD from your LUNCHBOX. Now go to 150.

'What an odd way to write,' said Anne when they had finally decoded the man's directions. 'Perhaps it's the only way they've been taught,' said Dick. But they also wondered whether The Barnies had just been playing a friendly joke on them. After all, they certainly seemed full of fun! *Go to 110.*

Just as they were about to leave the little shop, Dick noticed some maps on a shelf in the corner. 'They be the finest maps you'll ever see,' said the proud shopkeeper, 'drawn by my father with his own hand.' They opened one up. Yes, they certainly were very beautiful – and might be useful, too!

If you don't already have it, put the MAP CARD into your RUCKSACK. Now go to 275.

They still hadn't decided whose choice to follow when they were greeted by a man carrying some funny red baskets. He said they were for catching lobster. He then asked if he could be of any help in directing them. 'Yes, can you tell us the best way to the clifftops?' enquired Julian. 'Certainly, me lad,' the man replied, 'just head straight for that there radio mast.' They hadn't gone much further, however, when the radio mast disappeared! It had been hidden by a sudden mist from the sea. The only way to find it again was to look it up on the map.

Use your MAP CARD to find out which square the radio mast is in — then follow the instruction. If you don't have one, you'll have to guess which instruction to follow.

If you think D4	go to 83
If you think B3	go to 162
If you think E3	go to 130

'Oh, it's hopeless,' complained George, 'we'll never find it in this dark!' Julian suggested they have one more search, though. And they would probably do it a lot better after a little refreshment. They were all in favour of that idea!

Take one PICNIC CARD from your LUNCHBOX. Then go to 136.

On their way down again, George discovered a message scratched into the stone of the wall. When they brought their torches nearer, they saw that it was in code!

Use your CODEBOOK CARD to find out what the message said by decoding the instruction below. If you don't have one, go to 52 instead.

L p D R g M

Just as they were about to enter, Dick noticed some writing scratched into the wood. *JIM – WALK 40 PACES ROUND THE BUILDING* it read. 'Then someone *has* been recently!' Julian exclaimed. They decided to walk the forty paces to see what was there.

*Use your MEASURE CARD to measure these 40 paces —
then follow the instruction there. If you don't have one,
you'll have to guess which instruction to follow.*

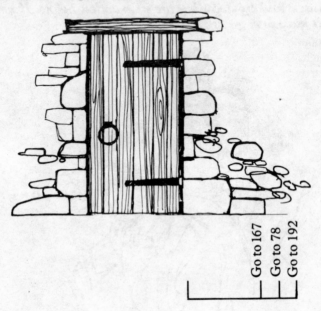

Go to 167
Go to 78
Go to 192

94

Suddenly, they heard a noise from the bottom of the stairs. Someone was there! They cautiously went back down to see who it was. But when they reached the house part again, whoever it was had gone. 'Perhaps it was just our imagination,' said Julian. Then Timmy started to sniff around an old cupboard. 'There seems to be something about this cupboard that's not right,' said George pulling open its doors. Inside, there was a large hole through the floor. Julian peered in to have a closer look. There were iron rungs all the way down. It was obviously the entrance to a secret passage! One by one, they climbed in. Just as they had reached the bottom of the shaft, they heard the noise again. It was directly above. The person was coming down after them! *Go to 295.*

95

Anne spotted some gulls flying above. It meant that the sea must be round any corner now. And also, perhaps, was the tower! First, though, they met a rather strange sight coming the other way down the road. It was a covered wagon with the word *'BARNIES'* written on it. Sitting on the wagon were some very jolly-looking people. All except one, that is, who seemed rather grumpy and unfriendly. The Five decided to run up to meet them.

Throw the FAMOUS FIVE DICE to decide who is to reach the wagon first.

JULIAN thrown	go to 37
DICK thrown	go to 117
GEORGE thrown	go to 277
ANNE thrown	go to 105
TIMMY thrown	go to 236
MYSTERY thrown	go to 215

96

Dick's idea worked! *TO THE COAST – 2½ MILES* the sign read. 'Once we reach the sea,' Julian said as they hurried along with excitement, 'finding the tower should be easy. It's bound to be near the coast – or the ships wouldn't have seen it.' *Hurry along with them to 287.*

Anne had only just started up the steep, rocky path when it began to rain. It was a very heavy rain, pelting against the cliff. 'Quick, we had better find somewhere to shelter!' she said, turning round to the others. But there didn't seem to be anywhere! Then Jan spoke, suddenly remembering something. His grandfather had once said there was a small place to shelter exactly 100 metres up. 'Clever boy, Jan!' they all said, patting him on the back.

Use your MEASURE CARD to measure this 100 metres – then follow the instruction there. If you don't have one, you'll have to guess which instruction to follow.

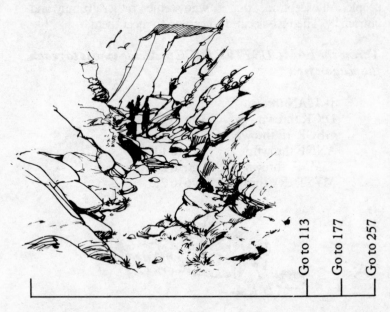

Go to 113

Go to 177

Go to 257

98

'What does anyone suggest now?' asked Julian when they found that their codebooks weren't the right type. 'Me know,' said Jan, pulling at his arm, 'me know the way.' Of course – they had completely forgotten about Jan! He had been living here all his life! 'We should have asked you earlier, Jan,' the others apologised as the little boy led the way. **Go to 5.**

Having followed Anne to the other side of the hole, they found that it was virtually impossible to see. 'We're going to have to use a torch,' she said. When they tried to switch the torch on, however, they discovered that the batteries were flat. They searched through their rucksacks to see if they had any spare ones.

Use your TORCH CARD to light up the way by placing exactly over the shape below. If you don't have one, go to 291 instead.

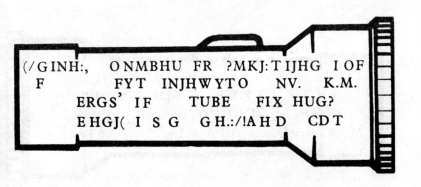

They at last found the right path and began to climb. They were nearly at the top when Julian tripped and dropped his lunchbox. There was the awful sound of a bottle breaking. That was obviously the end of his ginger beer!

Take one PICNIC CARD from your LUNCHBOX. Then continue to 30. (Remember: when there are no picnic cards left in your lunchbox, you must start the game again.)

The sky grew even darker and Dick was finding it more and more diffficult to see. He was becoming worried that the path might have crumbled away in some places and they wouldn't realise it until it was too late. They certainly wouldn't survive that long a fall! 'We had better use a torch,' he said, turning round to the others. They felt through their rucksacks to see if they had one that still worked.

Use your TORCH CARD to light up the way by placing exactly over the shape below. If you don't have one, go to 57 instead.

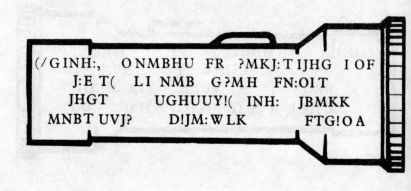

'Do you think you could still find the way without a torch?' the sergeant asked when they discovered that their batteries were flat. The rest of The Five couldn't but they were sure Timmy could! They set him on the scent, following right behind. And just to provide extra encouragement, George gave him some of her cake!

Take one PICNIC CARD from your LUNCHBOX. Now go to 86.

'We'll just have to do without the tunnel,' said George when they couldn't seem to find it. The wind was so strong and biting that it made her eyes water. She began to wipe them with a handkerchief but the wind suddenly snatched it out of her hand. It caught on a bush growing under a ledge a little further up. As she went to pick it up, she noticed that the bush was concealing a large hole! 'This must be the secret tunnel!' she exclaimed, leading them in. *Go to* **261.**

They were continuing on their way when Anne was suddenly drenched by a shower of water from the passage roof! They weren't sure whether it was a leak or someone had stored the water up there deliberately. Fortunately, her anorak was waterproof but the water had soaked the inside of her rucksack. 'That will teach me to do up the flap in future,' she laughed, checking the rucksack's contents. Everything else was fine but the map had become wet through! It was so soggy that she had to throw it away.

If you have one, take the MAP CARD from your RUCKSACK. Now to to 80.

105

'Pleased to meet you, madam,' one of the men greeted her as Anne ran alongside the wagon. 'We're travelling players,' he added, 'I hope you'll be able to come and see our show.' Anne said that she hoped so too, giggling at his funny costume. When she could finally stop the giggles, she asked if he knew how much further it was to the sea. 'Just beyond the ancient circle of stones,' he replied with a comical little bow.

Use your MAP CARD to find out which square the circle of stones is in — then follow the instruction. If you don't have one, you'll have to guess which instruction to follow.

If you think D2	go to 166
If you think D1	go to 12
If you think C2	go to 196

106

They were brought to another coded message! *KEEP TO THE FLOORBOARDS WITH A LARGE KNOT IN THEM* it read. 'Here's one!' cried Anne. 'And here's another!' cried George. They stepped from one to the next.

Step with them to 187.

'We had better be careful how we tread,' said Anne as they continued to climb in the darkness. Suddenly, the lid of her lunchbox fell open. The catch couldn't have been fastened properly. 'Oh no!' she exclaimed. 'I've lost some of my sandwiches.'

Take one PICNIC CARD from your LUNCHBOX. Now go to 290.

'And where might you be going?' the woodcutter asked them politely before they left. 'To the sea,' Julian replied, 'we want to do a bit of exploring.' The woodcutter gave a concerned frown. 'Well, mind you be careful of those caves,' he said, 'they can be very dark and dangerous.' He rummaged through the little knapsack he carried. 'Here, borrow this just in case,' he said, handing Julian a torch. 'When you've finished with it,' he added, 'you can leave it with one of the farmers. They all know me hereabouts.' Having thanked him, The Five continued on their way.

If you don't already have it, put the TORCH CARD into your RUCKSACK. Then go to 220.

'I'm glad we decided to let Timmy go first!' Julian whispered as they followed his white tail. Timmy was always a lot braver than the others. They had gone quite a long way along the dark passage when Anne noticed a small wooden door at the side. Behind it, there was a large cavern like a room! It was full of old chests and

crates. 'Look here!' shouted Dick, shining their torch at one of
them, 'there's a message on the lid.' When they bent a little closer,
however, they noticed that it was in code.

*Use your **CODEBOOK CARD** to find out what the mes-*
sage said by decoding the instruction below. If you don't
have one, go to 153 instead.

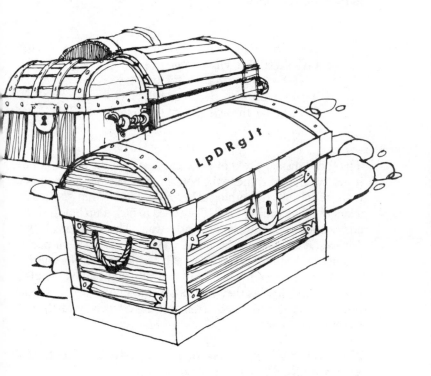

110

Climbing a small ridge, they at last arrived at the sea! There was a
huge sandy beach just beneath them. 'Now it should be easy to find
The Wreckers' Tower,' said Julian, 'all we have to do is go to the
cliffs!' They saw some in the distance and so they walked towards
them along the sand. On their way, they discussed The Barnies.

They all agreed what nice people they were – all except that grumpy one, of course. Anne said that she heard the others call him the Guv'nor and he seemed to be in charge. The cliffs were now very close and they discussed how best to climb to the top. They all had different ideas!

Throw the FAMOUS FIVE DICE to decide whose idea they should follow.

JULIAN thrown	go to 154
DICK thrown	go to 76
GEORGE thrown	go to 199
ANNE thrown	go to 10
TIMMY thrown	go to 271
MYSTERY thrown	go to 260

111

The coded message told of a secret passage at the bottom of the stairs. When they came to the bottom they searched all round but there was absolutely nothing to be found. Then Timmy sniffed out a length of measuring tape. They tried to pick it up but the other end seemed to be trapped under the wall. 'This must be it!' cried Julian suddenly, '– on the other side of here!' They all pushed against the stone and, slowly, part of it began to open. Not only had they found the secret passage but they also now had both ends of the measure! Just as they had put it into one of the rusksacks, however, they heard a noise from outside. Someone was coming towards the passage ...

If you don't already have it, put the MEASURE CARD into your RUCKSACK. Now go to 295.

George led them from the farm to a small signpost. 'I remember
seeing this last time we passed,' he said. They switched on their
torch so that they could read it. *FOR THE POLICE STATION* it
began ... but the rest of the direction was in code. 'This must be a
special signpost for policemen only,' said Anne, as they searched
their rucksacks for a codebook.

Use your **CODEBOOK CARD** *to decode the sign. If you
don't have one, go to 98 instead.*

FOR THE
POLICE STATION
L p A F

There wasn't time to look for the shelter, however, because a full
storm broke out, thunder echoing round the cliffs. Unless they
thought quickly, they were going to become soaked! 'I know,' said
George, 'let's put our lunchboxes over our heads.' At first, the idea

sounded rather funny but then the others realised how clever it was. So they quickly transferred their picnic to their rucksacks, opening the lunchbox lids to form a kind of hat. The 'hats' worked very well but, unfortunately, Anne dropped some of her sandwiches on the ground as she was transferring them. They were so wet and dirty that they had to be thrown away.

Take one PICNIC CARD from your LUNCHBOX. Now go to 240.

114

Not far from the lighthouse on the map was a twisting, yellow line leading up to the cliffs. They turned to the map's cover to find out what a yellow line meant. It meant a footpath! 'See, I told you it might help us find one,' said Dick as they began to follow it. On the way up, Timmy sniffed out something in the grass. It was a measure! They took it with them in case they needed a spare.

If you don't already have it, put the MEASURE CARD into your RUCKSACK. Now go to 30.

115

They followed the turning up a small hill. When they reached the top of the hill, they could see a little stone building below. The blue lamp at the front showed that it was the police station. They all ran down towards it. *Go to 35.*

They had gone a lot further along the passage when Julian
suddenly stopped. He had found a cigarette packet on the ground.
Turning it over, he noticed there was a message pencilled on to the
back. 'Maybe this is a clue as to who those men were!' he said
excitedly. But, unfortunately, the message was in code. They
would need one of the codebooks to read it.

Use your CODEBOOK CARD to find out what the
message said by decoding the instruction below. If you
don't have one, go to 225 instead.

'Hello,' said one of the men on the wagon, 'we're The Barnies.
We're a travelling pantomime group.' Dick replied that they would
very much like to see their show some time but, for the moment,

could they tell them how much further to the sea. 'Ay,' said the man helpfully, 'there's a short cut to the beach just ninety metres back down this road.'

Use your MEASURE CARD to measure the 90 metres —
then follow the instruction there. If you don't have one,
you'll have to guess which instruction to follow.

Go to 288

Go to 50

Go to 217

118

Dick discarded the rest of his sandwiches on the way. His lunchbox appeared to be growing heavier by the moment and it now made it a lot easier to run. It seemed a pity to throw away all Mrs Penruthlan's hard work but he was sure she wouldn't mind under the circumstances!

Take one PICNIC CARD from your LUNCHBOX. Now
go to 86. (Remember: when there are no picnic cards left in your lunchbox, the game is over and you must start again.)

Julian was right! The coded message told them to take the left branch. With Timmy taking the lead again, they continued in that direction. *Go to 178.*

'Here it is!' said Julian, pointing out a step that had almost completely crumbled away. They all went very carefully past it, continuing to feel their way round the wall. A little further up, George discovered that one of the stones in the wall was loose. They wondered whether it might be a secret hiding place. Julian eased the stone out, feeling inside with his hand. 'Yes, I've found something!' he said excitedly, bringing out a small rectangular object. It was a codebook!

If you don't already have it, put the CODEBOOK CARD into your RUCKSACK. Now go to 290.

The coded message told them to take the branch on the right. They had only gone a short way along it before Jan gave a loud scream! 'Look, a ghost!' he cried, pointing to a large white shape hovering above. The others all laughed kindly. 'Don't be silly!' Anne told him. 'It's just a seagull. It's just difficult to see because of the dark.' But Jan wasn't satisfied until Timmy had scared the bird away with a loud bark. *Go to 249.*

Dick suddenly noticed that Jan was missing. They were just beginning to worry about him when they saw his head pop out from the hole. While they were deciding who should go first, he had already done so! They crawled through the hole after him, Anne taking his hand again. A little further along the tunnel, they noticed a sheet of paper attached to the rock. *BEWARE POT-HOLE 90 METRES FURTHER ALONG* it read. Jan helped them look through their rucksacks for a measure.

Use your MEASURE CARD to measure this 90 metres — then follow the instruction there. If you don't have one, you'll have to guess which instruction to follow.

Go to 307

Go to 283

Go to 193

123

It took some while but finally they approached the light green summit. It also took several sandwiches!

Take one PICNIC CARD from your LUNCHBOX. Now go to 152. (Remember: when there are no picnic cards left in your lunchbox, you must start the game again.)

The idea seemed to work! When they had flashed back the signal, the boat continued on its way round the coast. 'What a relief!' said Dick, 'we could have been in real trouble then.' *Go to 92.*

The path took them very near to the cliff edge. They could see the sea crashing against the rocks below. They imagined how awful it must have been for those ships tricked by the flashing light. Suddenly, disaster happened! There was a huge gust of wind and it blew Julian's map out of his hand. The last they saw of it was as it dropped into the water way, way below!

If you have one, take the MAP CARD from your RUCKSACK. Now go to 312.

Just as they were leaving the church, Julian suggested checking where it was on their maps. 'They always show a church,' he said, 'and it might tell us how much further we have to walk.' The others agreed it was a good idea, beginning to look through their rucksacks.

Check to see if you have a MAP. If you have, use it to find out which square the church is in – then follow the instruction. If not, you'll have to guess which instruction to follow.

If you think B2	go to 95
If you think B3	go to 14
If you think C3	go to 139

Their torches were very good ones, with brand new batteries, and they lit up the whole of the floor. There was rubbish and dust everywhere. They were looking for the next patch of oil when their torches suddenly lit up a bright plastic circle. It was a measuring tape, obviously dropped by someone! They put it in their rucksacks as a spare before continuing on the trail.

If you don't already have it, put the MEASURE CARD into your RUCKSACK. Now go to 150.

128

The coded message told them that there was a key under one corner and they should use it to open the lid. 'Yes, here it is!' said Anne excitedly, finding a rusty piece of metal. They put it in the lock and turned. At first, it didn't look as if it would work but then the lid finally came open. They shone their torch inside. Lying right at the bottom was a sailor's map of the coast!

If you don't already have it, put the MAP CARD into your RUCKSACK. Now go to 49.

129

'Yes, a ford might be fine for vehicles to cross,' complained George, 'but how about us?' There was nothing for it but to take off their socks and shoes and wade across. 'Ouch!' yelled Anne, 'I've trodden on something.' Putting her hand into the water, she brought up what looked like an old measure. 'Well done, Anne!' laughed the others, 'that might come in useful as a spare.'

If you don't already have it, put the MEASURE CARD into your RUCKSACK. Now go to 275.

130

'Look, here it is!' said Julian, pointing out a small symbol on the map, 'we must continue straight ahead.' They were soon beginning to climb high above the sea and so it looked as if they were going the right way. 'Yes, there's the radio mast again!' exclaimed Dick as the mist suddenly lifted. It had become a lot bigger and closer now. *Go to 152.*

131

They suddenly forgot how many paces they had counted. 'We'll just have to start again,' said Anne. This time they were a bit more careful and they finally emerged by a pond. At one end of the pond, there was an old hut. 'It was probably used by fishermen to store their tackle,' said Julian. Then he thought he heard a noise from inside. They decided to investigate. *Go to 45.*

132

Now they had discovered where the light was flashed from, they decided to return to the bottom. Maybe there would be more clues as to who was responsible! *Go to 92.*

133

'It's definitely the tower!' Julian said with a shout for joy once they had decoded the message, 'I'm sure it is.' The others felt so too. They therefore hurried in its direction. *Hurry with them to 70.*

It took some while but finally they seemed to be on the right track. Anne was sure she could smell the sea in the air. So was Timmy – his nostrils twitching! Before any sea appeared, however, they came across a small church. The parson asked them if they would like to come in for some of his wife's lemonade. They were so grateful for the lemonade that they decided to offer them a gift for the church charity. 'Oh, thank you – that's most kind, most kind,' said the parson as he accepted George's torch.

If you have one, take the TORCH CARD from your RUCKSACK. Now go to 126.

They finally found the path to the top and began to climb. Suddenly, there was an explosion from George's lunchbox! The path was so steep and bumpy that it had fizzed up her ginger beer and blown the top off. There was only a tiny drop left at the bottom.

Take one PICNIC CARD from your LUNCHBOX. Then continue up the path to 30. (Remember: when there are no picnic cards left in your lunchbox, you must start the game again.)

Not long after, they passed an old wooden door. 'Imagine finding a door all the way down here!' exclaimed George. They decided to open it and look inside. It was a large room cut into the rock! They shone their torch round. It was full of old boxes and crates. They went to examine some of them but they were all empty. Suddenly, they heard a slamming noise from behind. Someone had shut the door on them! They ran up to it, trying to push it open, but it wouldn't shift. They were just about to see whether someone had put a key in the lock when their torch went out. Something was wrong with it! They quickly felt through their rucksacks for another one.

Use your TORCH CARD to light up the lock by placing exactly over the shape below ... then follow the instruction. If you don't have one, go to 273 instead.

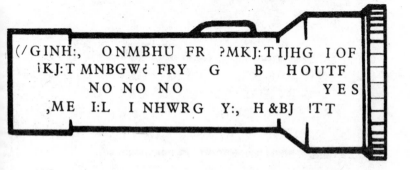

137

The map showed that they weren't that far from the police station after all! It was just round the next corner. They were just about to set off when George noticed something at the bottom of the sheep grid. She squeezed her hand in, trying to reach it. 'Oh, leave it alone George,' said Julian, 'we don't have much time!' George made one last effort and finally managed to bring it out. It was a codebook! She quickly popped it into her rucksack before running to catch the others up.

If you don't already have it, put the CODEBOOK CARD into your RUCKSACK. Now go to 5.

Much further along the passage, Dick heard a very faint ticking sound. It was coming from near his feet. Bending down to investigate, he discovered that it was a watch! 'This must have been dropped by one of those men Jan saw,' he said excitedly. He turned it over to find out if there was a name inscribed on the back. There was – he could feel the grooves! But he would need a torch to read it.

Use your TORCH CARD to read this inscription by placing exactly over the shape below .. then follow the instruction. If you don't have one, go to 36 instead.

```
(/GINH:,   ONMBHU  FR  ?MKJ:TIJHG  IOF
   WAS BVHUI  GUYR  H´XS?  GF
   RE      FKJH     G:ITRE     !QAU
   HT    GNB  IRFY& V EIN      HINJHE
```

Unable to see his map in his rucksack, Dick searched through his lunchbox. Perhaps he had put it in there by mistake! But there was only his picnic. 'Oh, look out!' Anne suddenly cried to him. He had left the lid off his lunchbox too long and some cheeky birds had come down and pecked at his sandwiches. 'That serves you right!' they all laughed.

Take a PICNIC CARD from your LUNCHBOX before going to 95.

'Oh, blow it!' said one of the men as their torch started to flicker. A moment later and it had completely gone out. 'This is our chance,' whispered Julian to the others, 'let's make a run for it.' By the time the men had put new batteries in, The Five were well and truly gone! *Continue along the tunnel to 175.*

'No, it's all right,' said Anne, not wanting to waste any time, 'I'll just try and be braver.' The others slapped her on the back for her courage. After all, she was the youngest! To help take her mind off it, Anne had some of her drink as she went along.

Take one PICNIC CARD from your LUNCHBOX. Now go to 152. (Remember: when there are no picnic cards left in your lunchbox, you must start the game again.)

142

'The trap must be about here,' said Dick when they had measured out the hundred metres. They felt around the passage floor for any secret button or trip-wire. 'Here it is!' cried Anne, finding a length of taut string about an inch above the ground. They pressed it with a stick they found. Suddenly a large hole opened just in front of the string! 'What a nasty trick!' said Dick as they all walked carefully round the edge. ***Go to 80.***

143

They quickly switched the torch on, continuing across the fields. On their way, Timmy discovered a map lying in the grass. There wasn't time to stop and put it in one of their rucksacks and so Timmy carried it in his mouth! Just as it occurred to them that they could use the map to help find the police station, Dick suddenly spotted it a few hundred metres ahead.

If you don't already have it, put the MAP CARD into your RUCKSACK. Now go to 55.

The coded message said that the goods were to be hidden near the shed until ready for collection. 'I wonder what shed it's talking about?' said Dick. They had only gone a few metres further along the tunnel when Anne noticed something else that had been dropped. It was a measuring tape with the name *JIM* stamped on to it! They put it into one of their rucksacks. Not only might it be useful but it would later be evidence for the police. They were absolutely convinced now that those men were doing something they shouldn't!

*If you don't already have it, put the **MEASURE CARD** into your **RUCKSACK**. Now go to 67.*

'Oh no, we must have come the wrong way!' exclaimed Julian as the path suddenly ended. A few metres further and they would have gone right over the edge! They went back the way they had come, finally reaching where the path had divided much further down. This time they took the other branch. Now they knew they were on the right track, they decided to have a quick bite to eat before continuing. All that wasted walking had made them hungry!

*Take one **PICNIC CARD** from your **LUNCHBOX**. Now go to 249.*

They suddenly heard a loud gasp from behind. It was Mrs Penruthlan! 'Heavens, where have you been all this time?' she exclaimed. 'I've been worried sick about you!' Julian replied that he would explain later but it was very important that she told them the way to the police station. 'The police station?' she considered, still in confusion, '. . . you just take the left turn 50 metres from the farm gate.'

Use your MEASURE CARD to measure this 50 metres — then follow the instruction there. If you don't have one, you'll have to guess which instruction to follow.

Go to 38

Go to 115

Go to 62

The others said it would be better to save their torches for later, however, suggesting they just feel their way along the wall. The wall was wet and slimy and the tunnel seemed to go on for ages. At last, however, they could see a tiny circle of light. They all rubbed their eyes as they stepped out. 'I hope we don't have too many adventures like *that*!' said Anne, happy to be able to see again. 'Woof!' Timmy agreed. ***Now continue on your way to 287.***

148

Next, they came to a window but it was boarded up. They found that the board came away quite easily, though, and it made the hole much lighter. They were now able to see a series of footprints in the dust and they decided to follow them. Before they started, they had a quick drink of their ginger beer.

Take one PICNIC CARD from your LUNCHBOX. Then go to 187.

149

The message directed them to the path and it wasn't much longer before they had left the wood behind. They were all pleased to be in the open again. All except Timmy, perhaps, who was still thinking about those squirrels. He was sure he could have caught them if they had stayed a bit longer! ***Go to 220.***

150

They finally came to a stone doorway at the far end of the room. Climbing over the tumbled-down door, they discovered a steep spiral staircase. It obviously led up to the tower! They prepared themselves for the long climb to the top.

Thrown the FAMOUS FIVE DICE to decide who is to lead the climb.

JULIAN thrown	go to 214
DICK thrown	go to 227
GEORGE thrown	go to 4
ANNE thrown	go to 303
TIMMY thrown	go to 172
MYSTERY thrown	go to 263

151

'Be careful you don't fall in!' George warned Timmy as he ran up and down at sight of the water. Timmy loved water. But it was too late. The next time they looked round, it was to the sound of an almighty splash! He had gone head over tail. 'It's a good job you can dry yourself quickly,' they all chuckled as he gave himself a brisk shake. ***Now continue on your way to 287.***

152

Only a few more steps to go and they were there – standing at the very top of the cliff! They could see for miles and miles but where

was the tower? Then Anne remembered something Jan's grandfather – the old shepherd – had told them. At the top was a heap of large rocks. If you walked exactly 70 metres from these rocks in line with the distant church, legend had it that you could see The Wreckers' Tower. Having found the heap, they quickly searched through their rucksacks for their measures.

Use your MEASURE CARD to measure the 70 metres from the heap of rocks – then follow the instruction there. If you don't have one, you'll have to guess which instruction to follow.

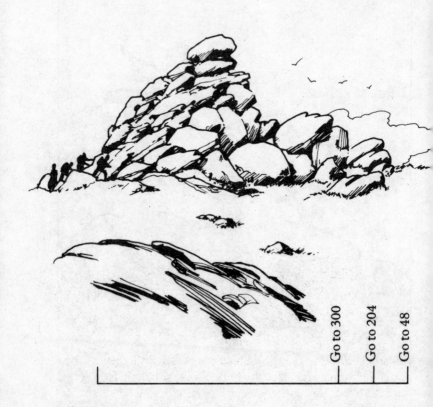

Go to 300

Go to 204

Go to 48

153

'Perhaps there will be another clue inside the chest,' Julian said, opening the lid. But it was completely empty, except for an old brass button right at the bottom. They decided to have some picnic to make up for their disappointment. They'd never had a picnic underground before!

Take one PICNIC CARD from your LUNCHBOX. Then go to 49.

154

Julian's idea was to keep going along the beach until they reached the cliff bottom. Then they might find some sort of path up. They hadn't gone far when they met some fishermen, mending their nets by their boat. Julian asked them if they knew of a way to the cliff top. 'Ay, young sir,' one of them replied. 'There's a little path cut into the rock just 140 paces from here.'

Use your MEASURE CARD to measure the 140 paces — then follow the instruction there. If you don't have one, you'll have to guess which instruction to follow.

Go to 135

Go to 238

Go to 282

On their way again, they passed a small grassy bank full of holes. Timmy suddenly darted towards one of them, poking his nose into the earth. 'Oh no, not again!' George cried wearily, 'Timmy – will you leave the rabbits *alone*?' They were all agreeing what a bad dog he was when he came trotting back with something. It was a code-book! 'Perhaps you're not such a bad dog after all,' George apologised, giving him a loving pat, 'and this codebook might well have a use.'

If you don't already have it, put the CODEBOOK into your RUCKSACK. Then go to 287.

Thinking that decoding it might waste too much time, they decided just to guess which path led upwards. They chose the left one. Unfortunately, they were wrong! After climbing for a bit, the path suddenly dropped down towards the cove on the other side of the cliffs. They were so tired by the time they reached the monument again that they decided to have a short rest before taking the correct path. Perhaps some ginger beer would be rather welcome too!

Take one PICNIC CARD from your LUNCHBOX. Then continue to 245. (Remember: when there are no picnic cards left in your lunchbox, you must start the game again.)

157

Julian went up to the little wall that stopped you falling over the edge. He very carefully leant over to see how far it was to the ground. He wasn't careful enough, though, because some stones suddenly gave way under his hand! Luckily, he just jumped back in time but he let go of the torch he was holding. It fell all the way to the bottom!

If you have one, take the TORCH CARD from your RUCKSACK. Now go to 92.

158

A good bit of walking later, The Five arrived at a deserted graveyard. It was in the middle of nowhere and the stones were very old. Many of them had sunk right into the ground. 'I expect this is where the local folk used to be buried,' said Julian, '– a long, long time ago.' They tried to read some of the inscriptions to find out the dates. 'Look, this is an odd one!' remarked Anne, 'it seems to be in some sort of code.'

*Use your **CODEBOOK CARD** to find out what the inscription said by decoding the instruction below. If you don't have one, go to 226 instead.*

L p D R g k F

159

The wagon had hardly turned the corner when one of The Barnies came running back. He said his name was Sid and he formed half of the show's pantomime horse! He then gave them a codebook, saying it might be useful for their adventure.

*If you don't already have it, put the **CODEBOOK CARD** into your **RUCKSACK**. Now go to 267.*

160

Half way round, George suggested that they have some of their ginger beer. The room was very dusty and it had made her throat dry. The others willingly agreed.

Take one PICNIC CARD from your LUNCHBOX. Now continue to 150.

161

Timmy ran up to the edge of the water, looking in. He suddenly jumped back in fright. Staring back was another dog - just like him. He slowly went up to the edge again and growled. The other dog growled too. Timmy growled even louder. No dog was going to outdo him, he thought. 'Come on, you silly old thing,' shouted George, 'it's just your reflection!' When Timmy has caught you up again **go to 287.**

162

It was such a steep walk that they decided to have a rest half way up. They watched the sea gulls swooping for food below. It made them feel quite hungry themselves and so they agreed to have some of their picnic. 'What delicious sandwiches!' said Anne as she munched on one made of ham and pickle.

*Take one **PICNIC CARD** from your **LUNCHBOX**. Now go to 312.* (Remember: when there are no picnic cards left in your lunchbox you must start the game again.)

163

They had gone a good way along the dark passage when they noticed a door built into the side. Behind it, there was a large underground cavern! 'It seems to be some sort of storage room,' said Julian, noticing all the old chests and crates. They decided to examine one of them but their torch had gone very dim. 'I know!' said Dick, having an idea, 'we'll light a piece of paper with some matches I brought.' He took a wad of paper from his rucksack, screwing it up tightly before lighting it. 'There – that's perfect!' he said. But just as the paper had finished burning, he suddenly realised what it was. He had accidentally set fire to his codebook!

*If you have one, take the **CODEBOOK CARD** from your **RUCKSACK**. Now go to 49.*

164

Since they couldn't find a torch quickly, they decided to wave instead. It seemed to do the trick, the boat continuing on its way. Just in case, though, they thought they had better return to the bottom. Anne kindly left the gulls some of her sandwiches before they went.

Take one PICNIC CARD from your LUNCHBOX. Now go to 92.

165

'I wonder whether he meant 110 of *our* paces or *his* paces,' said Julian when they still hadn't found a path. The gypsy's paces, of course, would have been a lot bigger! Finally they did find a path, however, and it led through fields and woods towards a small church. They decided to have a quick rest on the churchyard seat while they checked through their provisions. 'Oh no!' exclaimed George, 'I've left my torch on and the batteries have gone flat. Now we won't be able to use it.'

If you have one, take the TORCH CARD from your RUCKSACK. Now go to 126.

166

'Look, there it is!' George suddenly pointed ahead as a large circle of stones appeared. The stones were very worn and half covered by the grass. 'They probably date back thousands of years,' said Julian. When they had finished examining the site, they continued on their way. *Continue with them to 267.*

167

'It's another door at the back!' Julian exclaimed when they had reached exactly forty. This looked like a newer entrance, built specially. The inside was very dark and scary and cobwebs trailed from the ceiling. Anne suddenly noticed a used match on the floor. Then another, then another. It looked as if someone had been trying to light his cigarette. They decided to follow the matches to see where they went. Next to one of them, they also found a code-book! They took it with them in case it might be useful.

If you don't already have it, put the CODEBOOK CARD into your RUCKSACK. Now go to 187.

168

The writing was a lot brighter now! *THIS IS THE PROPERTY OF ABRAM TRELAWNY – 1874* it said. 'Goodness, that's old!' exclaimed Julian. 'This must be where the wreckers hid their plunder until it was safe to sell.' They opened the chest up to look inside but it was completely empty. ***Go to 49.***

George squeezed through the rotting door, the others following. It was very dark inside but they could just find their way. They wondered where the entrance to the tower was. Then they heard a sudden sound from the corner. 'What's that?' asked Anne in a fright. The sound came again. 'It's just a pigeon,' Julian reassured her as he realised what it was. That made him start to think. Since all the windows were boarded up, the only way the pigeon could have flown in was down through the tower! All they had to do was clap their hands and follow which way it escaped. But they would need a torch or they would never be able to see it.

Use your TORCH CARD to follow the pigeon's flight by placing exactly over the shape below. If you don't have one, go to 87 instead.

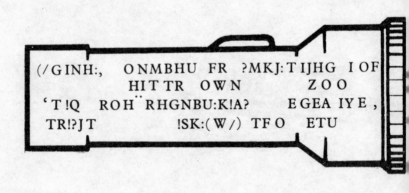

Luckily, the ledge was only a few metres down and Timmy had merely grazed his leg. George held the torch while Julian helped pull him up. 'Perhaps that will teach you a lesson!' George said when Timmy was safely back on the path again. But she was so pleased to find that he wasn't hurt that she couldn't really be that angry with him. 'And what's that you've got in your mouth?' she scolded, still pretending. It was an old measuring tape! He must have found it on the ledge when he had fallen.

If you don't already have it, put the MEASURE CARD into your RUCKSACK. Now go to 240.

171

They finally found the ruined castle. They decided to have a quick rest while they checked their equipment. 'Oh no!' Julian said suddenly, 'I've lost my codebook. It must have fallen out while we were looking for our maps.'

If you have one, take the CODEBOOK CARD from your RUCKSACK. Now go to 267.

172

With the others right behind, Timmy mounted the crumbling stone steps. It was very dark up the stairway but, finally, they came out into the open air at the top. The wind whistled all about them and gulls circled near their heads. Down below, they could just see a large cave at the bottom of the cliffs. 'I bet that's where they used to hide the plunder after the wreckage!' said Dick. They decided to look it up on the map in case they wanted to explore it later.

Use your MAP CARD to find out which square the cave is in – then follow the instruction. If you don't have one, you'll have to guess which instruction to follow.

If you think E4	go to 79
If you think A4	go to 157
If you think B4	go to 132

173

'There it goes!' cried Dick as the torch lit up the crab's sideways run. They chased after it, Timmy well in the lead. 'Oh, do be careful!' George warned him as he sniffed at its shell, 'it might pinch you!' The passage became more and more damp and they realised it couldn't be far to go now. Suddenly, Timmy turned his attentions from the crab to something else. He had found a ball of paper wedged into a crack in the passage floor. Carefully unfolding it, they saw that it was a map! Although it was a little damp, it was still perfectly readable and so they took it with them.

If you don't already have it, put the MAP CARD into your RUCKSACK. Now go to 80.

'What a shame we still couldn't make out the rest of that inscription,' Dick said as they stepped out into the open again, 'it might have saved us a lot of walking.' They wondered who could have written it. Perhaps it was the people who used to flash that dreadful light from the tower! Perhaps this was where they hid! All this wondering was making them hungry. They decided to make a short stop and sample some of Mrs Penruthlan's delicious picnic.

Take one of your PICNIC CARDS from the LUNCHBOX before continuing to 95.

After what must have been a whole hour in the tunnel, they at last saw a tiny ray of light ahead. It was coming from an open trapdoor in the roof. Leading up to the trapdoor was a ladder. They quickly climbed it, coming out into some farmer's shed. There were sacks of corn everywhere. Then Dick realised where they were! 'Why, it's our farmer's shed!' he exclaimed. 'Look, there's Mr Penruthlan's spare wellingtons!' Julian now thought he knew what those men were up to. They were probably smuggling drugs from another country. They would let the boat know that it was all clear to land by flashing a light from The Wreckers' Tower. Then they would come running down the underground passage to meet it. As soon as the drugs had been unloaded, they would be taken along The Wreckers' Way to this shed and then hidden somewhere nearby. 'What an ingenious idea!' exclaimed George, '. . . but we must stop them.' So they quickly piled sacks on to the trapdoor to keep the men inside until they had fetched the police. But they all had different ideas as to where the police station was.

Throw the FAMOUS FIVE DICE to decide whose idea to follow.

JULIAN thrown	go to 202
DICK thrown	go to 9
GEORGE thrown	go to 112
ANNE thrown	go to 229
TIMMY thrown	go to 81
MYSTERY thrown	go to 146

Following Dick through the hole, they soon came across a message painted on to the tunnel wall. *JIM – CODEBOOK HIDDEN BEHIND CROSS 130 PACES FURTHER ALONG* it read.

'That codebook must have some sort of use,' said George as they excitedly started to count the paces.

Use your MEASURE CARD to measure these 130 paces – then follow the instruction there. If you don't have one, you'll have to guess which instruction to follow.

Go to 67
Go to 292
Go to 241

177

The sky was becoming more and more stormy, the waves crashing against the rocks below. It wasn't long before they were wet through from the rain but they just could not find anywhere to take cover. 'We'll just have to keep climbing,' said George. 'Perhaps there will be somewhere further up.' They eventually found a small ledge just at the side of the path. It was by no means perfect but at least it kept most parts of them dry when they huddled underneath. It was only their feet that were still getting wet! They decided to have some of their picnic while they were waiting for the rain to stop.

Take one PICNIC CARD from your LUNCHBOX. Now go to 240.

178
The tunnel seemed to go on and on and, after a lot more walking, Julian suggested they should have a rest on a large rock. They hadn't been resting long when they noticed a light coming towards them from back down the tunnel. 'It must be those men!' said Anne with alarm. They quickly crouched behind the rock as the men came nearer. ***Go to 310.***

179
'The passage seems to be getting wider,' Julian shouted back to them as he led the way. They kept expecting it to end but it went on and on, further and further. It felt as if they were quite a long way

under the ground. Suddenly, their torch shone upon a coded message chiselled into the rock! 'Quick, let's look for a codebook,' Julian said.

*Use your **CODEBOOK CARD** to find out what the message said by decoding the instruction below. If you don't have one, go to 224 instead.*

L p Z R g W C

They saw the beach becoming smaller and smaller below. The wind blew stronger and stronger. It looked as if this *was* the way to the top! *Continue along this route to 312.*

'Yes, I think Anne's choice is best,' they finally agreed. It led them across a field and to an old signpost. 'What funny writing on it,' remarked Dick, 'it doesn't make any sense.' They all had a closer look. It was not in English, as you would expect, but in strange symbols. Then Julian suddenly remembered something Mrs Penruthlan had told him back at the farm. The Cornishmen of old often used to write their signs in a special code so outsiders would not be able to understand them. 'That must be why she gave us all a codebook!' Anne declared with delight.

Use your CODEBOOK CARD to find out what the writing said by decoding the instruction below. If you don't have a CODEBOOK, go to 264 instead.

'The key doesn't seem to be here,' sighed Julian after they'd been searching for nearly half an hour, 'perhaps it's already been taken.' They sat down on one of the chests, wondering what to do next. They would just have to hope that someone would come looking for them. 'Well, it's a good job we brought a picnic with us,' George said, 'I'm starving!' Timmy was half way through his slice of cake when he suddenly dropped it and leapt for the door. Someone was unlocking it!

Take one PICNIC CARD from your LUNCHBOX. Now go to 295. (Remember: when there are no picnic cards left in your lunchbox, you must start again.)

Whether they liked his choice or not, Timmy was going to take them *his* way! Running excitedly along, he led them to a large flat stone in the grass. 'Why it's only a stone!' the others all laughed. 'Why should we be interested in that?' But a little further along, he uncovered another – exactly the same. Then another, then another. 'It's obviously some sort of ancient path,' exclaimed Dick, 'and look – this one has some writing on.' The writing was very smooth and worn but they could just make out some strange symbols. 'It's in code,' realised Julian, 'let's look for our code-books.'

Use your CODEBOOK to find out what the writing said by decoding the instruction below. If you don't have a CODEBOOK, go to 73 instead.

'I'm sure it's this way,' said Dick as they all followed him. A lot of branches and cut legs later, though, and they were just as lost as before! They all had a rest while Julian looked through his rucksack. 'Perhaps the wood will be shown on the map,' he said, digging right to the bottom for it.

Use your MAP CARD to find out which square the wood is in – then follow the instruction. If you don't have a MAP in your RUCKSACK you'll have to guess which instruction to follow.

If you think B2	go to 248
If you think A3	go to 216
If you think C1	go to 296

185

It wasn't just the stairs the torch lit up but also a codebook! It was lying on one of the steps about half way up. They blew the dust off before taking it with them. It might be a different type to theirs!

If you don't already have it, put the CODEBOOK CARD into your RUCKSACK. Now go to 290.

186

They had just finished decoding the inscription when George's hand felt something amongst the long grass at the bottom of the stone. It was a measure! They put it in their rucksacks, thinking it might be useful later on. 'I wonder how it got there?' asked Anne. 'It must have fallen out of someone's pocket,' replied Julian, 'and you know what that means – *someone else has been this way!*' They all gave a little shiver at the thought before continuing.

If you don't already have it, put the MEASURE CARD into your RUCKSACK. Now go to 95.

The trail took them to an old fireplace at one end of the room. Timmy started to sniff around inside it – then he suddenly disappeared through the floor! It looked as if he had found some sort of secret hole. The rest climbed into the hole as well. There were iron rungs all the way down, forming steps for them to tread on. They soon came to the bottom of the hole, coming across a passage that seemed to lead under the building. They decided to see where it went.

Throw the FAMOUS FIVE DICE to decide who is to go first.

JULIAN thrown	go to 179
DICK thrown	go to 265
GEORGE thrown	go to 213
ANNE thrown	go to 44
TIMMY thrown	go to 109
MYSTERY thrown	go to 222

They didn't have to go far along the turning before they spotted the police station's blue lamp! They hurried in its direction. **Go to 55.**

'Its a good job we *did* have the right type of codebook,' George thought secretly as they followed the message's instruction. A little further on through the wood, they spotted a gypsy's caravan. It looked as if it had been abandoned there. Most of the paint had peeled off and weeds grew between the wheels. Then Julian thought he noticed someone at the window! They hurried towards it, climbing the steps. **Go to 45.**

190

Timmy had taken them some way further along the passage when he sniffed out a piece of broken mirror. 'Fancy leaving that here,' said Anne, 'someone could have hurt themselves on it!' She was just about to put it into her rucksack to find somewhere safe for it later, when she noticed some writing on it. It had been done with a wax pencil. The trouble was that it was in code!

Use your CODEBOOK CARD to find out what the writing said by decoding the instruction below. If you don't have one, go to 104 instead.

191

'We must have passed it,' said Anne. 'It's probably easy to miss in this dark.' They then decided to let Timmy try and find it. But he wouldn't move! At first they wondered what was wrong with him, then George suddenly realised. 'O.K.,' she laughed, patting him on the head, 'you can have some cherry cake before you start!'

Take one PICNIC CARD from your LUNCHBOX. Then go to 136.

Half way round, they forgot how many paces they had counted and had to start again. The second time they counted more carefully and arrived at another door at the back. This one opened much more easily. The inside was very dark and dingy and cobwebs trailed everywhere. Suddenly, Timmy seemed to sniff out a scent on the floor! It led towards the next room. **Go to 187.**

193

Since they couldn't find a measure quickly, they decided they had better tread carefully for the next few minutes. The ground wasn't very easy to see in this darkness and a pot-hole could be dangerous. **Go to 307.**

194

'The tunnel obviously runs for quite a distance,' said Julian as they put the map away. They started walking more quickly, worried that they were never going to reach the other end. **Go to 67.**

Timmy began to sniff among the stones and rubble at their feet. 'What is it, Timmy?' the others asked. He sniffed right up to the little wall that stopped you falling over the edge. 'Oh, do be careful!' said George, 'that wall doesn't look very safe.' Suddenly he started to dig through the stones with his paw. He had found a torch!

If you don't already have it, put the TORCH CARD into your RUCKSACK. Then go to 92.

196

On their way, Timmy suddenly thought he saw a rabbit! He rushed past Anne's legs. It took her so much by surprise that she dropped her torch. When they unscrewed the top, they found that the bulb had broken.

If you have one, take the TORCH CARD from your RUCKSACK. Now go to 110.

197

'Those old Cornishmen were certainly very clever,' said Dick, once they had deciphered the message. 'Yes - and very distrustful of outsiders,' added Julian with a laugh. The signpost pointed them to a small country road. They were a little way along it when they met a tinker coming from the other direction. 'Would you like to buy any of my wares?' he asked, showing them the tray that rested at his waist. They sifted through the knick-knacks and the old toys and coins. Anne found a torch. 'Does it work?' she asked. 'As good as the day it was new,' he replied with a proud smile. 'In that case we'll buy it,' she chuckled, handing him the money.

If you don't already have it, put the TORCH CARD into your RUCKSACK. Then go to 287.

198

They then tried to open the chest up but they didn't have any luck! The lid was well and truly locked. 'Oh well, at least it makes a nice seat to have our picnic on!' said Anne. They all agreed, feeling quite hungry after their long walk down the passage.

Take one PICNIC CARD from your LUNCHBOX. Now go to 49.

199

George led them to a triangular stone standing just back from the sand. Chiselled into one side there were some strange symbols. 'I bet this tells the way to the clifftop,' said George, 'but they put it in code so only the wreckers would understand.' The rest agreed. After all, the wreckers would hardly want the police knowing how to reach the top! The Five then looked for their codebooks to decode the instruction.

Look for yours too. If you don't have a CODEBOOK, go to 123 instead.

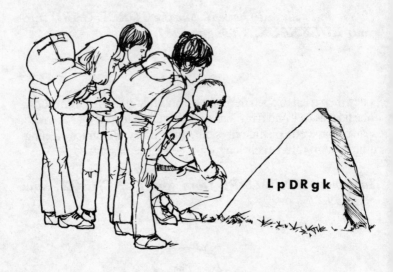

L p D R g k

Just as they were about to leave the river, George noticed something shiny in the water. At first she thought it was just a fish but then she realised it was a bottle. It had a cork in it and inside there was a book! They excitedly fished the bottle out, wondering what the book could be. 'Look, it's a codebook!' exclaimed Dick as they opened the pages, 'let's take it with us.'

If you don't already have it, put the CODEBOOK CARD into your RUCKSACK. Now go to 158.

'Are you sure you know where you're going?' Julian asked as they followed George into a wood. 'Of course,' she replied, 'I'm a better pathfinder than any of you boys.' But as the wood became thicker and thicker, darker and darker, George began to wonder herself. She daren't admit to the others that she was lost, though. They would never let her hear the last of it. Timmy suddenly stopped at a tree, scratching away at the moss. Carved into the bark was a coded message! 'See, I told you we'd find some sort of clue this way,' George bragged – but then she had an awful thought. Did they have the right type of codebook with them?

Use your CODEBOOK CARD to find out what the message said by decoding the instruction below. If you don't have a CODEBOOK CARD in your RUCKSACK, go to 134 instead.

L p D R g k C

202

'I'm sure it's this way,' said Julian as they all followed him on a short cut across the fields. Suddenly, though, the moon disappeared behind a large cloud and they could no longer see. They quickly searched for a torch in their rucksacks, knowing that they didn't have much time.

*Use your **TORCH CARD** to light up the way by placing exactly over the shape below. If you don't have one, go to 60 instead.*

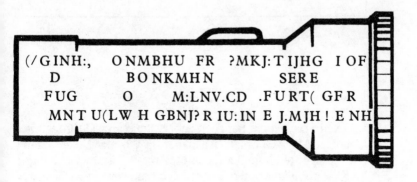

203

Much further along the passage, Anne noticed some writing chalked on to the wall. *BEWARE TRAP 100 METRES FURTHER ON* it read. 'It must be to stop people snooping about,' said George. They wondered what the trap would be. They didn't really like the thought of it. 'It's a good job we have our measures with us,' said Dick.

Use your MEASURE CARD to measure the 100 metres to the trap – then follow the instruction there. If you don't have one, you'll have to guess which instruction to follow.

Go to 104

Go to 281

Go to 142

204

Unable to see hers in her rucksack, Anne searched through her lunchbox. Maybe she had put it in there by mistake! No, she hadn't but the sight of all that delicious food made Timmy feel hungry. 'O.K., Timmy,' the others laughed, 'you can have a slice of cherry cake. In fact, we all will!' As they were eating their picnic, Dick suddenly spotted something poking out from behind a ridge below. It looked like the top of a flagpost. Perhaps it belonged to The Wreckers' Tower! They hurried towards it.

Take one PICNIC CARD from your LUNCHBOX. Then go to 70.

205

'Does anyone have any other ideas?' asked Julian when they found that the sheep grid wasn't shown on their maps. Then Timmy suddenly started barking at the top of his voice! 'Oh, how can that help, you silly thing?' chided George. But it wasn't long before another dog started barking back. It sounded like the deep, strong bark of an Alsatian. 'Why, it's the police dog!' Dick suddenly realised, 'it's Timmy's clever way of finding the station.' George decided that Timmy wasn't such a silly thing after all. Nothing like it! *Go to 5.*

206

It was growing darker by the minute and the path was becoming more and more difficult to follow. Suddenly, a seagull flew out in front of them and the shock made George lose her balance! Luckily the others were just able to catch her in time but her rucksack slipped off her shoulders. It caught on a ledge a few metres below. The others held on to Dick's legs as he tried to rescue it. He finally managed to lift it up by the strap but the measure fell out just before he brought it to safety.

If you have one, take the MEASURE CARD from your RUCKSACK. Now go to 249.

They continued to climb, noticing that the sea was becoming more and more rough as it grew darker. 'I hope there aren't any boats out,' said Dick, as the waves crashed against the rocks below. ***Go to 240.***

On all fours, they followed Julian into the dark interior. Then the tunnel became a lot higher and they were able to stand up. They hadn't gone much further before Dick discovered a piece of paper on the ground. It was a navigation chart showing where all the rocks were around the cove. And at the top there was scrawled a coded message!

Use your CODEBOOK CARD to find out what the message said by decoding the instruction below. If you don't have one, go to 63 instead.

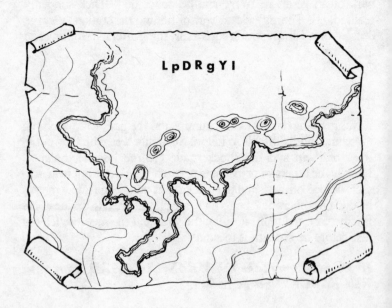

Just as the situation was beginning to look desperate, Anne had a second idea! She silently opened her lunchbox, taking out the ginger beer. After pushing up the cork until it was nearly out, she gave the bottle a furious shake. There was a loud bang as the ginger beer exploded, ehoing round the tunnel. It sounded just like a gun! In the men's confusion, The Five made their escape. 'Let's just hope there isn't much further to the other end,' said Julian, as they hurried along.

Take one PICNIC CARD from your LUNCHBOX. Now go to 175.

210

They could now hear the splash of the waves ahead. 'Only a little bit further,' Anne said to Jan, giving his hand an encouraging squeeze. He didn't like the dark very much. *Go to 40.*

211

Julian's choice led to a small country road. It twisted and turned before, finally, it came to a river. There was no bridge across the river. It just flowed straight across the road! They all wondered how vehicles were meant to pass. Then Dick suddenly realised. 'It's called a ford,' he explained, 'the water is so shallow that they can drive straight through.' Julian thought for a moment. 'And it might also be a clue to where we are,' he added, 'something as unusual as this is bound to be shown on the map.' So they all opened their rucksacks to take their maps out.

If you have a MAP in your RUCKSACK, use it to find out which square the ford is in – then follow the instruction. If you don't have a MAP, you'll have to guess which instruction to follow.

If you think A3	go to 151
If you think B3	go to 161
If you think B1	go to 129

212

Ahead, they spotted the clifftops. They were nearer than they thought! 'Yours wasn't such a bad way after all, Anne,' Julian told her. There was more good news. Dick suddenly felt an odd shape in his pocket. He dug his hand in, wondering what it could be . . . *he* didn't remember putting anything there! It was a codebook with "To Dick" written on the front. Mr Penruthlan must have slipped it in as a present!

If you don't already have one, put the CODEBOOK CARD into your RUCKSACK. Then go to 245.

'I wonder how much further it goes?' George asked as she led the way. The passage seemed to run for miles, twisting and turning through the underground rock. They must have left the tower behind long ago. Suddenly, they came across a message chalked on to the passage roof. It had partly been washed out by some dripping water but they could just about read the words: *JIM – HIDING PLACE IS THROUGH HOLE IN ROCK 80 METRES FURTHER UP.*

Use your MEASURE CARD to measure the 80 metres — then follow the instruction there. If you don't have one, you'll have to guess which instruction to follow.

Go to 191

Go to 247

Go to 91

Julian led the way up the narrow, crumbling steps. They were a part of the way up when Dick noticed a message chalked on to the wall. It read: *BEWARE THE DANGEROUS STEP 30 PACES UP.*

Use your MEASURE CARD to measure these 30 paces — then follow the instruction there. If you don't have one, you'll have to guess which instruction to follow.

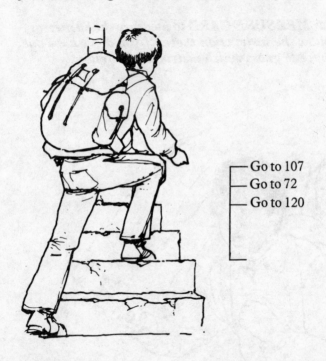

— Go to 107
— Go to 72
— Go to 120

'We're The Barnies,' the men called from the wagon, 'come and see our show!' After they had thrown them a leaflet to say when they would next be performing, the wagon disappeared on its way. 'Look, their next show is tomorrow,' read Julian excitedly, 'and it's to be in the barn of our farm!' For the moment, though, they still had to find the sea and they wondered which way to go. 'The sea's over there,' a small, mysterious voice cried suddenly. For a long time they couldn't work out where the voice was coming from but then they noticed a tiny figure in the trees above. It was the little boy, Jan! 'The sea's over there!' he repeated. But he was so hidden by the leaves that they couldn't tell which way he was pointing. They would have to shine a torch on him.

*Use your **TORCH CARD** to find out where Jan is indicating by placing exactly over the shape below. If you don't have one, go to 12 instead.*

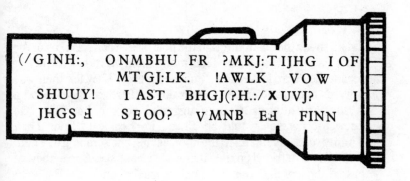

216

They were hardly started again when Dick tripped on a large stone. Luckily, he wasn't at all hurt but the contents of his rucksack rolled down a bank and into some nettles! They were able to retrieve most of them with a stick but his measure lay right in the centre. It was impossible to reach it without badly stinging themselves and so they decided they would just have to leave it.

*If you have one, take the **MEASURE CARD** from your **RUCKSACK**. Now go to 158.*

217

They found a winding, stony path. The stones looked like the stones from a beach and so they were sure they must be very close now. ***Go to 110.***

218

Julian shone the beam through the hole. 'Yes, I can see a key at the other end!' he exclaimed. That made them all rather uneasy. It meant they were locked in ... maybe for ever! They felt their way towards one of the crates and sat down. 'Perhaps they'll send a rescue party after us,' George suggested, not very hopefully. She knew the passage would be almost impossible to find. Then Timmy suddenly ran up to the door, licking and scraping it. There seemed to be a friend on the other side. 'Look,' said Anne, 'they've passed the key underneath.' They hurriedly put it into the lock, eager to see who this friend was ...

Go to 295.

Having found the radio mast on the map, they looked to see if it was higher than the ground around. It was! They therefore decided to walk to it. It was quite a long walk but they didn't mind all that much since they had some good fortune on the way. Anne spotted a codebook lying in the grass! Then she spotted something else. Not far below them was the top of a small round building. Could it be The Wreckers' Tower at last?! They all broke into a run towards it.

If you don't already have it, put the CODEBOOK CARD into your RUCKSACK. Now go to 70.

A little further along, they came across a signpost. *FOOTPATH TO THE SEA: 100 METRES* it read. When they ran ahead to find it, however, they discovered there were three footpaths – all next to each other! 'Which do we take?' asked Anne. Julian had a think for a moment. 'The only way to be sure,' he replied, 'is to measure out the hundred metres exactly.' They therefore looked through their rucksacks for their measuring tapes.

Use your MEASURE CARD to measure the 100 metres from the signpost — then follow the instruction there. If you don't have a MEASURE CARD, you'll have to guess which instruction to follow.

Go to 293

Go to 54

221

But then Julian thought it might be dangerous even with a torch and said that they had better stay where they were until the storm passed. 'Never mind, it won't take long,' he reassured them, 'and, luckily, there's no rain with it.' To cheer themselves up, they had some of their picnic.

Take one PICNIC CARD from your LUNCHBOX. Now continue to 245. (Remember: when there are no picnic cards left in your lunchbox you must start again.)

While they were still deciding who should go first, Anne noticed a
drawing chalked on to the passage wall. It showed that the passage
led through the cliffs and came out not far east of a wooden cross.
They decided to look up the cross on the map to see how far away it
was.

*Use your MAP CARD to find out which square the cross is
in – then follow the instruction. If you don't have one,
you'll have to guess which instruction to follow.*

If you think A4	go to 163
If you think C4	go to 75
If you think D4	go to 28

Since no further flashes appeared, they just had to guess where the
first one came from. They thought a small dip in the cliffs to
the right might be a likely place. You could just about hide a tower
there. Before they went any further, though, they decided to have a
quick drink of their ginger beer. The salty air had made them all
thirsty!

*Take one PICNIC CARD from your LUNCHBOX. Now
go to 70.* (Remember: when there are no picnic cards left in your
lunchbox you must start the whole game again.)

224

Continue along the underground passage to 136.

225

Jan started to tug at George's elbow. 'Me hungry,' he said, 'me want cake.' George gave him a cross look, saying it was rude to ask for things. 'Oh, don't be so mean, George!' laughed the others. 'Just think how helpful he's been!' George soon changed her mind, though, giving him the largest slice she had. After all, the poor scamp did look very thin.

Take one PICNIC CARD from your LUNCHBOX. Now go to 40.

226

'Oh well, if we can't work out the code,' said Julian after several minutes of trying, 'at least let's have some picnic.' They didn't really fancy eating it in the graveyard and so they found themselves a nice patch of grass in a neighbouring field. 'This cherry cake is delicious!' remarked Dick, munching on one of Mrs Penruthlan's very generous slices. Timmy thumped his tail. He seemed to think so too!

Take one of your PICNIC CARDS from the LUNCH-BOX. When you have finished eating, go to 95.

The stairs were very narrow and dark and it was almost impossible for Dick to see. 'We had better use our torches,' he said, turning round to the others.

Use your TORCH CARD to light up the way by placing exactly over the shape below. If you don't have one, go to 46 instead.

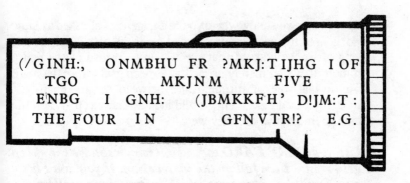

```
(/GINH:,    ONMBHU  FR  ?MKJ:TIJHG  IOF
    TGO        MKJNM        FIVE
  ENBG    I  GNH:    (JBMKKFH'  D!JM:T:
  THE FOUR   IN      GFNVTR!?    E.G.
```

'It looks as if we're just going to have to make a run for it,' whispered Dick when there was no sign of the men leaving. They waited until the men were looking the other way and then they suddenly darted out! As they were running, George accidentally dropped some sandwiches from her lunchbox. Seconds later, there was a deafening crash from behind. The men must have slipped on the butter as they were trying to catch them up!

Take one PICNIC CARD from your LUNCHBOX. Now continue along the tunnel to 175.

'Are you sure you know where you're going?' they all asked as Anne led them on to a nearby country road. She said that she did but, not long after, she realised that she was lost. Instead of the police station, they had merely arrived at a sheep grid across the road! Timmy had to be careful not to fall in between the bars. Then Dick suddenly had an idea. They could look up the sheep grid on the map to find out where they were.

Use your MAP CARD to find out which square the sheep grid is in – then follow the instruction. If you don't have one, you'll have to guess which instruction to follow.

If you think C2	go to 5
If you think A2	go to 137
If you think B3	go to 205

They were part way up the steep narrow path when it divided. Julian decided on the left branch, which circled a large flank of chalky rock. Half-way round, he noticed a tiny island just out to sea. It was really little more than a heap of rocks but he thought it might possibly be shown on the map. If it was, it would be a clue to where they were. They therefore looked through their rucksacks to see if they had a map with them.

Use your MAP CARD to find out which square the island is in – then follow the instruction. If you don't have one, you'll have to guess which instruction to follow.

If you think E4	go to 8
If you think B4	go to 206
If you think C4	go to 145

231

They were still deciding who should lead when Jan noticed a small crab further along the passage! 'It must have come up from the sea,' said Julian. That gave him an idea! If they followed the crab, they would be able to find their way to the other end. Suddenly, though, the crab shot away into the darkness. They would need a torch to find it again.

Use your TORCH CARD to follow the crab by placing exactly over the shape below – then follow the instruction. If you don't have one, go to 59 instead.

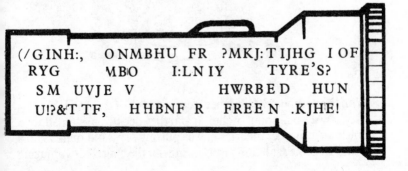

(/GINH:,   ONMBHU FR ?MKJ:TIJHG I OF
RYG   MBO   I:LN IY   TYRE'S?
SM UVJE V   HWRBED   HUN
U!?&T TF, HHBNF R   FREE N .KJHE!

'There it goes!' cried Anne as the pigeon rose into the air. It flew into the next room and then quickly disappeared. But it just gave them enough time to observe its route. 'This way!' said Julian, excitedly leading in that direction. **Go to 150.**

They had finally found the path and were nearing the top when they met a strange sight. There were some goats grazing on the grassy slope ahead. They went to stroke them, Timmy seeming particularly fascinated with the animals. The goats were very inquisitive, poking their heads into The Five's rucksacks. 'Oh no!' exclaimed George suddenly, 'this one's eating my map.' By the time they had freed it from him, there was only a tiny piece left!

If you have one, take the MAP CARD from your RUCK-SACK. Now go to 30.

With the codebook's help, they were soon out of the wood. Nearby, they saw a small country church and they decided to stop off for a quick look. Inside, the parson was putting some old things into a box. 'Hello,' he said, 'I'm just clearing out the church. It's amazing how much people leave over the years.' He added that he would probably sell what he found at the church jumble sale, giving the money to charity. 'In that case,' said George, looking through his box, 'perhaps we could buy this measure from you? A spare might come in handy.'

If you don't already have one, put the MEASURE CARD into your RUCKSACK. Now go to 126.

235

'Well, it looks as if we're going to have to go Timmy's way,' they all laughed as he suddenly dashed ahead of them. They weren't sure if he had sniffed out the right path or it was just rabbits he was after. Half an hour later, it became quite obvious which! 'There's that stone bridge again!' George exclaimed, tired out. 'Naughty Timmy,' the other three added, 'you've just taken us round in a big circle.' Timmy did not seem too bothered by the rebuke, though, just disappointed that he hadn't caught anything. 'Well, this time we're jolly well going to use our maps,' Julian told him crossly.

If you have a MAP in your RUCKSACK, use it to find out which square the stone bridge is in — then follow the instruction. If you don't have a MAP, you'll have to guess which instruction to follow.

If you think E1	go to 155
If you think A1	go to 77
If you think D1	go to 264

236

Timmy chased alongside the wagon, wagging his tail. The others arrived soon after, greeting the men 'Good morning.' 'Good morning to you too,' one of them replied, 'we're The Barnies - a travelling show.' That gave Julian an idea. If they did a lot of travelling, they'd probably be able to direct them. 'Are we going the right way for the sea?' he asked. They all nodded. 'Just take the little footpath 150 paces further along this road,' they said.

Use your MEASURE CARD to measure these 150 paces – then follow the instruction there. If you don't have one, you'll have to guess which instruction to follow.

Go to 12

Go to 159

Go to 286

237

Anne noticed that some of the floorboards had an extra nail at one end. 'Perhaps this is to mark out some secret route,' she said and they decided to follow them. Suddenly, there was a scream! George had mistakenly trodden on one of the rotten floorboards and fallen through! Faithful Timmy helped pull her out. Fortunately, she wasn't hurt but she had dropped some of her sandwiches in the fall. They had gathered so much dust that they had to be left.

Take one PICNIC CARD from your LUNCHBOX. Then go to 187.

238

'. . . 138, 139, 140,' they counted. And there the path was, winding its way to the top! They slowly made the stiff climb. ***Go to 312.***

239

They all followed Julian into a large field. Right at the other end there appeared to be a scarecrow. They could see this small shape in ragged clothes. When they looked again, however, it had moved! 'What can it be?' asked George as the scruffy figure came towards them. 'Why, it's Jan!' exclaimed Dick, 'he seems to pop up all over the place.' Letting him have a quick play with Timmy, they asked

Jan if he could show them the way. 'Only if me can see your torch,' the little scamp artfully replied, 'Jan never seen torch.'

Lend Jan your TORCH by placing card exactly over the shape below. He will then tell you the way to go! If you don't have a TORCH CARD in your RUCKSACK, go to 71 instead.

```
(/GINH:,  ONMBHU FR  ?MKJ:TIJHG  IOF
      TWA TWA G:I        HG  WOT?
   F RE!QS  IUH GNB BJG       UYR!  X/
YHINS S   ER      HIHI FU(L XERG IN
```

240

They all suddenly jumped with fright. A light started to flash from above! It could only be The Wreckers' Tower. They watched the light's ghostly reflection on the water, beginning to believe that the tower really was haunted after all. 'Look!' cried Dick, suddenly noticing a small motor boat on the waves, 'it's luring those people into the rocks.' They frantically waved their hands as a warning but the boat didn't appear to see them. 'Oh, I can't bear to watch!' said Anne, covering her eyes. When she opened them again, however, she was surprised to see that the boat had steered safely right into the cove. There was another surprise. Some men had come running from the secret passage to meet it. They now seemed to be unloading some packages from it. When they had finished, the men started to make their way towards the bottom of The Five's path! *Go to 311.*

241

'I can't see any cross,' said Anne when they had reached the last pace. Nor could the others. Then Jan found a tiny chalk mark on the wall. 'Here it is!' he said, showing them the minute blue cross. They noticed that the stone there was rather loose. A whole chunk came away in Julian's hands and behind it he found a polythene bag. Opening it up, he produced the codebook!

If you don't already have it, put the CODEBOOK CARD into your RUCKSACK. Now go to 67.

242

The coded message said that the boat would be bringing the goods from France! 'I wonder what goods it's talking about?' asked Anne mysteriously. They continued along the passage, hoping there would be further clues at the other end. ***Go to 80.***

243

'I wonder who could have written that inscription?' George asked as they took the route it suggested. 'Perhaps it was someone who discovered the wreckers' secret,' replied Julian, 'but they were too scared to tell anyone. So they wrote it down for others to investigate.' Whoever it was who had written it, The Five were jolly glad that they had! It could well save them a lot of walking! **Continue along this short cut to 95.**

244

Anne was just about giving up hope when she saw a man through the trees. 'He must be on the path,' she said, 'we've found it again!' Running over to him, sure enough they found the path. 'Hello, there,' said the man through his thick, dark beard, 'I'm the wood-cutter hereabouts.' Timmy started to lick his hand. That showed that they could trust him – so they asked him how much further to the way out. 'Exactly 120 paces from this tree,' he replied with a chuckle, 'I do it every day.'

Use your MEASURE CARD to measure these 120 paces – then follow the instruction there. If you don't have a MEASURE CARD in your RUCKSACK, you'll have to guess which instruction to follow.

Go to 131

Go to 84

Go to 108

'Do you think we've reached the very top?' George asked when it looked as if they couldn't climb any further. It certainly seemed so. The rocks looked tiny below and the wind really was quite strong. But they thought they had better somehow make sure. After all, it was only from the very top that they would get a good chance of spotting the tower. And, now they came to think about it, perhaps that radio mast over there was higher! 'I know!' said Julian, having an idea, 'we'll look it up on our maps. They always give heights as well.'

Use your MAP CARD to find out which square the radio mast is in – then follow the instruction. If you don't have one, you'll have to guess which instruction to follow.

If you think D4	go to 48
If you think E3	go to 219
If you think D3	go to 204

In the end, however, they decided not to risk the tunnel, turning back towards a small church. They remembered seeing a gardener in the churchyard as they passed. 'Hello,' said Julian, 'I wonder if you could tell us the way to the sea?' The gardener wiped his brow with a handkerchief before answering. 'I'm afraid I don't rightly knows,' he replied, 'I be new here since this morning.' But he wished them luck – saying he felt like a nice cool dip in the sea himself! *Go to 126.*

It wasn't very easy but at last they found it. There was a small gash in the rock wall to the left. 'A good job we have measures,' said Dick, 'or we would have walked right past it.' One by one, they squeezed through the narrow gap to the other side. ***Go to 136.***

248

Finally emerging from the wood, they spotted a small church on a hill. 'Let's climb up to it,' suggested Julian, 'we might get a view of the sea.' When they reached the church, however, they were to be disappointed. There were too many other hills in the way. ***Go to 126.***

249

They suddenly noticed a bright light flashing from above. They wondered what it was and then George realised! 'It's coming from The Wreckers' Tower!' she exclaimed with fear and excitement. Moments later, they saw a motor boat on the choppy sea below. 'The light must be luring it into the cliffs!' said Dick with horror. They watched helplessly as it came nearer and nearer to the rocks but it somehow managed to steer right through them and into the cove. Then something even stranger happened! Several men came running out of the secret passage to meet it. It looked as if they were unloading something from the boat's cabin. When the unloading had finished, the boat chugged back into the sea and disappeared in the direction it had come. The next thing The Five knew, the men were heading towards the bottom of their path! *Go to 262.*

250

In the end they decided to take the right branch of the river. Further along they met a solitary fisherman sleeping by his line. 'W-w-what's happened?' the fisherman asked as he awoke, thinking he had caught a fish. 'It's only us,' The Five laughed, 'we're sorry for disturbing you.' The fisherman started to chuckle too and, seeing he was friendly, they asked him if he had caught anything. 'Only this silly old book,' he replied, showing it to them. Dick turned the soggy pages. 'Why it's a codebook!' he exclaimed. The fisherman said that if it was of any use to them, they were more than welcome to it.

If you don't already have it, put the CODEBOOK CARD into your RUCKSACK. Now go to 220.

251

'What's that!' cried Anne as they saw a shadow ahead. They quickly shone their torch at it but it had gone. A few steps further and they saw it again! 'Oh, I knew we shouldn't have come this way,' said Anne. They all froze as the shadow started to come towards them. It seemed very small and thin. 'Do you think it's a ghost?' asked Dick in a shiver. ***Turn to 275.***

252

They followed Dick into the middle of a small, decaying room. Weeds grew through the floorboards and the paper hung in long tatters off the walls. They looked for the entrance to the tower part of the building but it was nowhere to be found. Then Anne noticed some writing on the faded wallpaper. It was very small and done in pencil. It read: *TO ENTER THE TOWER, GO 60 PACES ROUND THESE WALLS.*

Use your MEASURE CARD to measure these 60 paces — then follow the instruction there. If you don't have one, you'll have to guess which instruction to follow.

Go to 305
Go to 285
Go to 160

253

They hadn't gone much further when they heard someone panting behind them. It was the gypsy, trying to catch them up! They went back to meet him. 'Before you goes,' the gypsy said, showing them a map, 'you might like this as well.' They thanked him for it, giving him a coin in return. 'It looks a lot better than ours,' Julian told him as they said goodbye again.

If you don't already have it, put the MAP CARD into your RUCKSACK. Now go to 158.

254

Anne had taken them a good half way up when there was a sudden thunderstorm! Everywhere went very dark. 'Ooh, I'm a bit scared,' said Anne, 'I can't see where I'm treading. Say we go too near the edge?' Julian agreed that it could be dangerous and said they had better use their torches. As best they could in the bad light, they searched through their rucksacks for them.

Use your TORCH CARD to light up the way by placing exactly over the shape below. If you don't have one, go to 221 instead.

```
(/GINH:,   ONMBHU  FR  ?MKJ:TIJHG  I OF
     STEIN      :LNV.W  O    ETU   LN
   JNM:          MNBGEAZ!Q        .CD
  JHYO TR         RONO        J.MNH(E)
```

255

Timmy jumped through the gap, the others a little more hesitant behind. The inside was very dark and the floorboards creaked and groaned wherever they walked. Some of them were quite clearly rotten. They found their way into the next room. This was even darker and they totally lost their direction. 'I wonder which side of the building this is?' Julian asked, reaching a wall. Then he noticed a small hole of light in the stone. Through it, he could just see the top corner of a windmill sail in the distance. If they could find the windmill on the map, it would tell them which direction the wall was facing.

Use your MAP CARD to find out which square the wind-

mill is in – then follow the instruction. If you don't have one, you'll have to guess which instruction to follow.

If you think C3   go to 13
If you think B3   go to 148
If you think D3   go to 237

256

The path they decided on eventually took them to an old signpost by a deep, muddy pond. The signpost was so rotten, however, that the piece with the direction on had broken off. It now lay at the bottom of the water! 'It's too deep to reach,' said Dick, after trying to fish it out, 'and the water's so muddy it's impossible to read.' Then he had a brilliant idea. If they could put a torch under the surface of the water, it might just light up the letters.

Use your TORCH CARD to light up the signpost's direction by placing exactly over the shape below. If you don't have one in your rucksack, go to 32 instead.

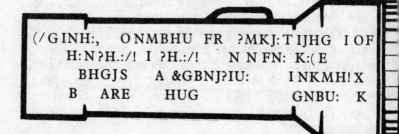

257

They found a tiny cave in the rock. It was just big enough for them all to squeeze in. They looked out across the dark sea, waiting for the rain to stop. 'I bet it was just such a night that the wreckers used to do their foul business,' said Julian. They could almost picture the poor ship struggling amongst the rocks. It was really quite eerie! *Go to 240.*

258

'Oh, what are we going to do?' wailed George when they heard another whine. 'I'll just have to go down to him,' said Julian, taking off his rucksack. He very carefully climbed down the rock. What seemed like hours later, he appeared again – with Timmy at his side! 'He's just scratched his leg,' he said. 'It was shock more than anything else.' George happily opened her lunchbox, handing Timmy a large slice of cake. 'You don't really deserve it,' she said, 'but it's great to see you again.' Timmy gave a bashful wag of his tail!

Take one PICNIC CARD from your LUNCHBOX. Now go to 240.

259

One by one, they followed George inside. Fortunately, the tunnel soon became wider and they were given more room. They no longer had to walk in single file. Suddenly, Jan noticed a scrap of paper on the ground. It was a plan of the tunnel, showing where it went. At one part, it ran directly under a church. They decided to look the church up on their maps to have some idea where they were going.

Use your MAP CARD to find out which square the church is in – then follow the instruction. If you don't have one, you'll have to guess which instruction to follow.

If you think B3	go to 194
If you think C2	go to 34
If you think C3	go to 67

'Hello, children!' they were greeted by a plump, elderly woman with a kindly face. She had suddenly appeared from behind them and asked if she could be any help. 'Yes,' said Julian politely, 'can you tell us the way to the clifftops?' She shook her head with regret. 'It be such a time since I last went,' she said, 'that I'm afraid I no longer remember.' She added that her husband would probably know but that he was a fisherman and was out in his boat at the moment. She pointed to it - a tiny speck far out to sea. Then she had a brilliant idea! They could flash the question to him in morse code with a torch. He knew morse code very well and he had a torch with him in his boat - so he could flash back the reply.

Use your TORCH CARD to find out the fisherman's

instruction by placing exactly over the shape below. If you don't have one, go to 100 instead.

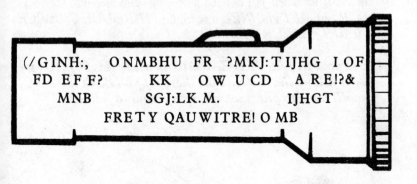

(/GINH:, ONMBHU FR ?MKJ:T IJHG I OF
FD EF F?   KK   O W U CD   A RE!?&
MNB   SGJ:LK.M.   IJHGT
      FRE TY QAUWITRE! O MB

261

The tunnel seemed to go on for ages and they wondered where it would come out. They must have gone quite a long way inland by now. Suddenly, they heard a sinister voice from behind! 'We know you're there,' it said, 'we found a map on the bush. One of you must have dropped it as you crawled through the hole.' The Five all looked at each other in panic. 'Come on!' said Julian, starting to run, 'we had better hurry before those men catch us up.'

If you have one take the MAP CARD from your RUCKSACK. Now go to 175.

'Quick, let's hurry!' said Julian as the strangers started to climb, 'I'm sure they can't be up to any good.' They had just turned the next corner when Jan noticed a message chiselled into the rock. *FOR SECRET TUNNEL*, it read, *GO THROUGH CREVICE 90 METRES FURTHER UP.*

Use your MEASURE CARD to measure this 90 metres — then follow the instruction there. If you don't have one, you'll have to guess which instruction to follow.

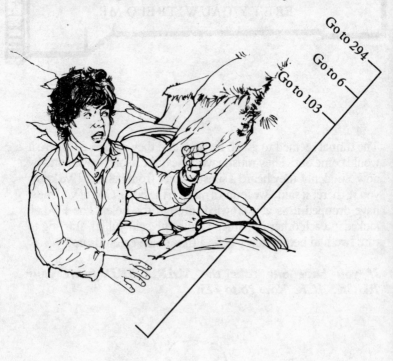

Go to 294

Go to 6

Go to 103

They suddenly heard a cry from the top! 'It sounds as if someone's in trouble!' exclaimed Julian, 'let's go and see if we can help.' They climbed as fast as they could up the narrow, dark stairs. Soon they were stepping out into the open air at the top. But there was no one there! Then they heard the cry again. 'It was just a seagull,' laughed Dick, pointing to the large white bird above', 'we're much too jumpy for our own good!' Julian didn't hear him, though, noticing something strange out to sea. Someone was flashing a light at them from a boat. He quickly showed the others. 'They're probably the people who still use the tower,' he said, 'and have spotted us up here. They must think we're part of their gang.' They wondered what they could do to prevent them from becoming suspicious. Then George had an idea. They could flash the same signal back with one of their torches!

*Use your **TORCH CARD** to see if the idea works by placing exactly over the shape below — then follow the instruction. If you don't have one, go to 164 instead.*

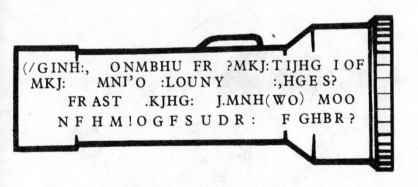

(/GINH:,   ONMBHU FR ?MKJ:TIJHG I OF
  MKJ: MNI'O :LOUNY   :,HGE S?
      FR AST   .KJHG: J.MNH(WO) MOO
  N F H M !O G F S U D R :   F GHBR ?

264

They hadn't gone much further before they decided to have some of their picnic. 'I could just do with something to eat,' said Dick, 'I feel as if I haven't eaten for days.'

*Take one of your **PICNIC CARDS** from the **LUNCH-BOX**. Then continue to 275.*

The passage seemed to go on for ever, twisting and turning through the rock. Dick turned round to ask the others whether they thought they should continue. 'Certainly,' they replied, 'we're not giving up now we've come this far!' A little later, their torch lit up a message chiselled into the rough, dark wall. It read: *FOR SECRET HIDING PLACE, TAKE BRANCH TO THE RIGHT 70 METRES FURTHER UP.*

*Use your **MEASURE CARD** to measure the 70 metres — then follow the instruction there. If you don't have one, you'll have to guess which instruction to follow.*

Go to 91

Go to 301

Go to 191

'You've played with it long enough now,' said George when Jan had had her torch for a good five minutes, 'you'll waste the batteries.' Jan wouldn't give it back, though, delighting in the way it switched on and off. In the end, they had to snatch it from him. 'I'm sorry, Jan,' said Dick, 'but we might well need it for our adventure.' Jan was so upset that he ran off in a sulk. They thought they had better go after him before he fell into any trouble. 'I think he went to into that barn,' said Julian, pointing towards the next field. *Go to 45.*

Crossing one more field, they at last came to the sea! 'Look, there are the cliffs!' cried Dick, pointing to some jagged white rocks in the distance. They looked cruel and treacherous. The Five immediately started walking towards them, knowing that The Wreckers' Tower would be somewhere near. On their way, they talked about The Barnies and what good fun they were. 'But I didn't like that grumpy-looking one,' said George. 'He must have been in charge because I heard the others call him the Guv'nor.' They assumed that he was grumpy because of all his responsibility. The cliffs were a lot nearer now but they weren't sure which route to take to the top. Each had a different choice!

Throw the FAMOUS FIVE DICE to decide whose choice they should follow.

JULIAN thrown	go to 297
DICK thrown	go to 24
GEORGE thrown	go to 304
ANNE thrown	go to 254
TIMMY thrown	go to 183
MYSTERY thrown	go to 90

'That's better!' said Anne, as the tunnel lit up all around them. 'It was a good job you brought a spare battery, Dick,' she added.

Continue along the tunnel to 178.

The coded message told them to look for a shrub a little further up. 'There it is!' cried George, pointing out this thick bush growing under a ledge. But they certainly couldn't see any tunnel! Then Timmy started to sniff at it, forcing his way through the branches. It concealed a large hole in the rock! They quickly crawled through. 'I wonder where this tunnel leads?' asked Dick when there still seemed no sign of it ending. They seemed to have been going along it for ages. Then they suddenly heard voices a long way behind. 'Oh no!' said George, 'those men obviously know about the tunnel as well!' ***Go to 175.***

'Before we go a step further,' Anne insisted 'I think we should stop and give Jan some of our picnic.' The rest agreed. It was the least they could do after Jan had been so thoughtful. And it looked as if he hadn't eaten for days. He soon made up for it, however, gobbling his way through three large pieces of cake!

Take one PICNIC CARD from your LUNCHBOX. Now go to 40.

Timmy bounded ahead towards a small tablet of stone in the grass.
Pulling the grass back with his paws, he revealed some writing on
it! 'Look!' exclaimed George, 'It's one of those old milestones.
Clever boy, Timmy.' They knelt down to read what the milestone
said but it was not like any ordinary milestone. It was more like a
riddle! *IF YE SEEK THE PATH TO THE TOP,* it read, *GO
EXACTLY 90 PACES TOWARDS THE NEEDLE. THEN, AS
IF BY MAGIC, THE PATH WILL APPEAR.* 'I wonder what the
needle is?' asked Dick. They were just about giving up, thinking it
didn't make any sense, when Anne noticed a very thin, sharp rock,
poking out of the sea. It looked just like a needle! They quickly
started pacing towards it.

*Use your MEASURE CARD to measure these 90 paces –
then follow the instruction there. If you don't have one,
you'll have to guess which instruction to follow.*

Go to 135
Go to 233
Go to 2

George led them round one tree and another until they discovered
the path again. 'Good ol' George,' they all cheered, 'we knew she
could do it.' As for Timmy, he gave her an affectionate lick! A little

further along the path, Timmy started to sniff out a strange tree trunk. It was completely hollow! 'Hey, look!' exclaimed Dick, poking his head inside, 'there's some sort of message carved into the wood!' The trouble was it was too dark inside the tree to read properly.

Use your TORCH CARD to light the message up by placing exactly over the shape below. If you don't have a TORCH in your RUCKSACK, go to 43 instead.

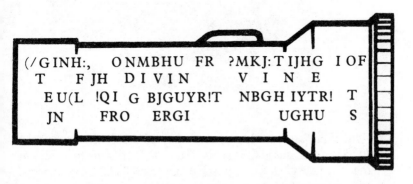

273

Just as they were looking for another torch, however, they heard the lock being turned from the other side. Someone was releasing them! ***Go to 295.***

274

'What do we do now?' asked Dick when their search for the key proved unsuccessful. They felt their way towards one of the crates and sat down. 'We'll just have to hope that someone comes looking for us.' Julian said. He knew there wasn't much chance, though.

Probably very few people knew of the secret passage. Not *good* people anyway! Some time later, however, they heard a noise from the other side of the door. Someone was turning the key! They were in such a hurry to reach it that Anne tripped on the way and lost her codebook.

If you have one, take the CODEBOOK from your RUCK-SACK. Now go to 295.

275

'Jan! What are you doing here?' they all asked at once as they suddenly recognised the grubby little boy. 'I've come to show you the way,' he replied with a mischievous grin. 'Well, just go straight back home,' George told him sharply, 'and don't you come creeping up on us like that again!' Frightened by her cross voice, Jan immediately disappeared. Now that he had gone, however, The Five started to feel rather guilty about him. 'After all,' said Anne, 'he was only trying to help – and maybe he *could* have shown us the way.' In fact, they needed him earlier than they thought for the path they were on very soon ended. It had become overgrown with branches.

Throw the FAMOUS FIVE DICE to decide who is to choose the way this time.

JULIAN thrown	go to 239
DICK thrown	go to 302
GEORGE thrown	go to 201
ANNE thrown	go to 23
TIMMY thrown	go to 309
MYSTERY thrown	go to 299

George immediately suggested another idea, however, to save time. Timmy could sniff out the patches of oil while they held on to his tail. His nose was just as good as any torch! On the way, however, Dick had a misfortune. He slipped on one of the oil patches and dropped his map. There wasn't a hope of finding it again in that darkness.

If you have one, take the MAP CARD from your RUCKSACK. Now go to 150.

'What does *The Barnies* mean?' George asked the man who was guiding the horse. 'That's us,' he replied cheerfully, 'we're called that because we perform shows in people's barns.' George asked whether they would be performing in Mr Penruthlan's barn. 'Most certainly, lad,' the man answered. George was so pleased that he thought she was a boy that she decided to ask him the way to the sea. The man wrote down the directions for them on a piece of paper. After the Barnies had disappeared round the corner, however, Julian noticed that the directions were written in a code.

Use your CODEBOOK CARD to decode the writing — then follow the instruction. If you don't have one, go to 50 instead.

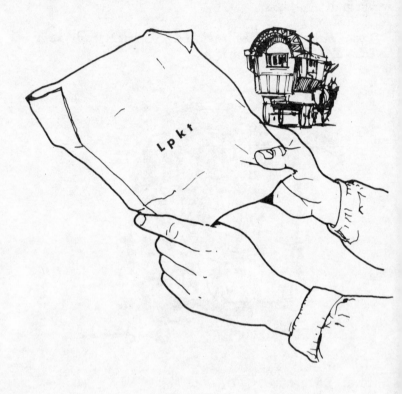

'A good job we had codebooks with us,' said Julian as they took the path the monument indicated. They were soon nearing the top. *Go to 30.*

The coded message told them that they were exactly half way to the secret cavern. 'This is beginning to sound exciting!' said Dick as they hurried along. They hadn't gone much further, though, before he suddenly stopped. He felt something crisp under his feet. Picking it up, he realised it was a map! They looked at the date on the cover. It was only one year old. That meant that someone had been down here very recently indeed!

If you don't already have it, put the MAP CARD into your RUCKSACK. Now go to 136.

280

First it was Julian who reached the other bank, then Anne, then Dick. George was about to step from the last stone when she stumbled! Luckily, she just managed to stop herself falling in but she dropped her torch.

If you have one, take the TORCH CARD from your RUCKSACK. Now go to 220.

281

Suddenly, a large hole opened in the passage floor! Jan nearly fell in but the others were just able to grab him in time. 'That must have been the trap,' said George once they were all safely past. Jan was so shaken by the nasty surprise that they gave him some of their picnic to make him feel better. Three slices of cherry cake later and he looked a lot happier!

Take one PICNIC CARD from your LUNCHBOX. Now go to 80.

The path must have been very hidden because they just could not find it anywhere. 'Let's go back and ask the fishermen if they will show us,' suggested Dick. The fishermen were only too happy to help, pointing out some narrow steps half-concealed by a rock. The Five were so grateful that they offered them some of their sandwiches. 'You can have ham, egg or sardine,' said Anne. Being fishermen, they all chose sardine!

Take one PICNIC CARD from your LUNCHBOX. Then climb the path to 30. (Remember: when there are no picnic cards left in your lunchbox, you must start the game again.)

'There it is!' said Dick, pointing out a deep hole in the ground. He dropped a pebble down it. He counted more than five seconds before they heard a splash. It must have been very deep indeed! They stepped very carefully round it and continued on their way. ***Go to 178.***

'O.K., we'll go your way, Dick,' the rest of them finally agreed. The path soon led to a tunnel, running under an old railway line. 'Ooh, it looks rather spooky,' said Anne, 'perhaps we should turn back.' They could hear the slow dripping of water inside and there was no sign of the other end. 'We'll be fine if we keep very close together,' said Julian uncertainly and they went cautiously to the entrance. 'I vote we use a torch as well!' added George, searching through her rucksack.

*Use your **TORCH CARD** to light up the way by placing exactly over the shape below. If you don't have one in your **RUCKSACK**, go to 147 instead.*

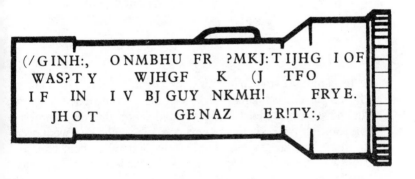

Pacing out the distance, they went round and round the room several times. 'What a funny instruction!' remarked Anne. 'It's probably to make sure the tower's difficult to find,' said Julian. At last they reached pace number 60. It had nearly brought them back to where they had started from! 'I don't see any tower here,' said Dick, 'it's just the same wall!' Then he noticed some tiny red dots painted on to the wallpaper. The dots led into the next room, then into a third room that they hadn't noticed before. It was very small and looked as if it had once been the kitchen. ***Go to 150.***

They certainly found *one* footpath but they weren't sure whether it was the right one. There was no sign of any sea! 'Perhaps we didn't count the right number of paces,' suggested George. They all agreed that they should go back and check that it wasn't another path they should have taken. On the way, Julian slipped in some mud and dropped his lunchbox. Some of his sandwiches were so dirty that they had to be thrown away.

Take one PICNIC CARD from your LUNCHBOX. Then go to 110.

After climbing a small hill, their track led into a wood. 'Hey, look at those squirrels!' exclaimed Dick, pointing high into a tree, 'let's go and have a closer look.' As they moved nearer the tree, however, the squirrels jumped into the next one. When The Five went over to that, they did it again! They started following them around, from one tree to another. 'Oh, this is hopeless!' panted Anne, 'we're never going to catch up with them.' When they turned round to join the path again, however, it was gone. They had strayed further than they thought. Each had a different suggestion as to how they might re-find the path.

Throw the FAMOUS FIVE DICE to decide whose suggestion to follow.

JULIAN thrown	go to 19
DICK thrown	go to 184
GEORGE thrown	go to 272
ANNE thrown	go to 244
TIMMY thrown	go to 74
MYSTERY thrown	go to 47

They climbed over a stile, following a tiny path through some fields. A lot of walking later, though, and there was *still* no sign of the sea. Perhaps this wasn't the short cut after all! They decided to look for another route. Before they went a step further, though, it was agreed that they should have some of their picnic. They needed a rest!

Take a PICNIC CARD from your LUNCHBOX. Then go to 267.

289

'Look, there's Julian's torch flashing!' exclaimed George, 'that must mean it's safe!' They had gone a bit further when they saw it flash again. 'It must be safe all the way,' said Anne with relief. ***Keep climbing to 312.***

290

They reached a small window in the wall. It was very long and thin like those in old castles. Through it, they could see a large building with a tall brick chimney at one side. 'It's an old copper mine,' explained Julian, 'there used to be quite a lot of them round here.'

They decided to look it up on their maps to see which direction they were facing.

Use your MAP CARD to find out which square the copper mine is in – then follow the instruction. If you don't have one, you'll have to guess which instruction to follow.

If you think C2	go to 52
If you think B2	go to 31
If you think D3	go to 94

291

They couldn't find any spare batteries, though. Fortunately it didn't matter because Timmy suddenly found a candle on the ground. And next to it there was a box of matches! 'Well done, Timmy!' the others said as they carried the candle in front of them up the tunnel. They had only gone a short way, however, when Julian thought he heard a voice from behind. 'Perhaps the men have come into the tunnel as well,' he said anxiously. They tried to think of a way to slow them up. 'If only we had some string,' said Dick, 'then we could make a trip-wire.' George scratched her head for a moment. 'I know!' she exclaimed, 'we can use my measuring tape.' So they hurriedly tied the tape across the ground.

If you have one, take the MEASURE CARD from your RUCKSACK. Now go to 178.

292

They had still to find the codebook when Julian decided that they couldn't waste any more time. 'Those men might be right behind us,' he said. 'We must get moving before they catch us up.' **Go to 67.**

293

Some distance further, they decided to stop for some refreshment. The sun was very hot and they were really quite thirsty! 'I can't wait to try some of that delicious ginger beer,' said Dick. At the mention of ginger beer, Timmy's tongue started to hang out. It looked as if he couldn't wait to try it either!

Take a PICNIC CARD from your LUNCHBOX. Now go to 95.

294

They at last found a narrow hole in the rock. It was almost completely hidden by brambles and moss. Just as they were about to enter, however, a whole flock of seagulls arrived. They started making the most awful shrieking noises. 'If they don't stop soon,' said Dick anxiously, 'they're going to give us away to the men.' First, Timmy tried growling at them but it had no effect. Then Julian had a better idea. Opening his lunchbox, he took out some of his sandwiches and threw them to the bottom of the cliff. The gulls immediately flew after them and left them in peace!

Take one PICNIC CARD from your LUNCHBOX. Now go to 175. (Remember: when there are no picnic cards left in your lunchbox, the game is over and you must start again.)

295

It was so dark that they couldn't quite work out who it was at first. He was very small and with a dirty face. Then they realised! 'Why, it's Jan!' they all shouted with delight on recognising his cheeky grin, 'what on earth are you doing here?' Jan told them that he had wanted to join their adventure and so he had run to the tower ahead of them. When he had arrived there, however, he saw some nasty-looking men flashing a lamp from the top. He became scared and ran away. But then he thought The Five might need his help and so he returned a little later. 'That was very thoughtful of you, Jan,' they all said, smiling at him. They decided he wasn't such a nuisance after all! Then Julian asked him if he knew where the passage went. 'Yes,' he replied, 'down to the sea. My grandfather told me about it.' The Five made up their minds to explore further!

Throw the FAMOUS FIVE DICE to decide who is to lead them.

JULIAN thrown	go to 116
DICK thrown	go to 138
GEORGE thrown	go to 85
ANNE thrown	go to 203
TIMMY thrown	go to 190
MYSTERY thrown	go to 231

'What's wrong?' asked the others when they noticed Anne looking back. 'There's a hole in my rucksack,' she replied, 'and I've dropped my measure.' They helped search the ground with her. 'It's no good,' said George when they had retraced some of their steps, 'even Timmy can't find it.' They therefore accepted that it was lost and continued on their journey.

If you have one, take the MEASURE CARD from your RUCKSACK. Then go to 158.

Julian's route led them higher and higher, further and further above the sea. But then the path they were on suddenly divided. One obviously went to the top and the other down to the bottom again. The problem was: which was which?! It was impossible to tell for the moment. Then they noticed a tiny stone monument a little further along. 'Why should anyone put a monument in such a deserted place as this?' asked Julian. 'I bet it's really a clue to the right path to the top.' They therefore examined it, looking for some sort of inscribed message. 'Yes, I was right!' cried Julian excitedly, 'look here – near the base!' But when they inspected the writing more closely, they found that it was in code.

Use your CODEBOOK CARD to decode the secret message. If you don't have one, go to 156 instead.

298

The idea worked! The light flashed again! It came from behind a small ridge at the other end of the cliffs. With Timmy in the lead, they hurried excitedly towards it. ***Go to 70.***

Still wondering which way to go, they noticed an old gypsy coming towards them. He had a spotted scarf round his neck and a big gold hoop in his ear. At first he looked rather scary but, as he came closer, they saw he had quite a friendly face. 'Good day to you!' Julian greeted him, 'can you tell us the way to the coast?' The gypsy gave them a big kind smile. 'Of course, me dears,' he replied, 'you walk 110 paces from that tree stump over there and that will set you right.'

Use your MEASURE CARD to measure the 110 paces — then follow the instruction there. If you don't have one in your rucksack, you'll have to guess which instruction to follow.

Go to 165
Go to 253
Go to 134

While they were measuring the distance, George suddenly discovered something on the ground. It was a map! 'Someone must have dropped it along the beach,' said Dick, 'and it was blown up here by the strong wind.' Putting it in one of their rucksacks in case a spare might be useful, they then continued measuring the seventy metres. Exactly on the seventy, Julian spotted the top of an old building showing behind a ridge below. Might it be The Wreckers' Tower? They all hurried towards it to find out.

If you don't already have it, put the MAP CARD into your RUCKSACK. Now continue to 70.

Having found the branch, they started to follow it. It was a lot narrower than the main passage and they hoped that it would soon lead into somewhere else. *Go to 136.*

Dick led them, via a twisting path, to a hill. At the top of the hill there was a small wooden bench for travellers to rest. They were just about to sit down when Anne noticed an inscription on it. *IF YE WISH TO GLIMPSE THE SEA,* it read, *GO EXACTLY 60 METRES ALONG THE LINE OF THE OAK.* 'I wonder what oak it's talking about?' asked Julian. For a while they were completely baffled, then George pointed to something on a neighbouring hill. 'Look, it must be that,' she said, showing them a solitary tree, 'it's the only oak to be seen.' They now knew which way to point themselves, but how were they to work out the 60 metres? They searched through their rucksacks for a measure.

Use your MEASURE CARD to measure the 60 metres from the bench – then follow the instruction there. If you don't have a MEASURE CARD in your RUCKSACK, you'll have to guess which instruction to follow.

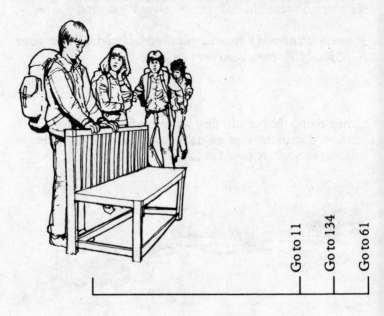

Go to 11

Go to 134

Go to 61

303

They all followed Anne up the narrow, crumbling steps. The climb seemed to last for ages but they finally came out at the top. They could see for miles and miles all around and the wind whistled through their hair. 'This must be where the wreckers flashed the light from,' said Julian, '... but I wouldn't like to be up here on a dark, stormy night!' Down below, they could see a small wooden cross near the cliff's edge. 'I bet that's in memory of the sailors who died here,' said Dick. They decided to look it up on the map in case they should ever want to come to the tower again. It might make it easier to find next time.

Use your MAP CARD to find out which square the wooden cross is in – then follow the instruction. If you don't have one, you'll have to guess which instruction to follow.

If you think C4	go to 195
If you think D4	go to 157
If you think E3	Go to 79

304

They followed George towards a battered signpost. The sign was very old and it was in the shape of a pointing finger. They could just about read the writing. *WAY TO THE CLIFFTOPS – 100 METRES ON* it read.

Use your MEASURE CARD to measure this 100 metres – then follow the instruction there. If you don't have one, you'll have to guess which instruction to follow.

Go to 125   Go to 83   Go to 53

Halfway round, Anne suddenly tripped over George's feet and dropped her lunchbox. Some of her cake fell out. 'Oh well, at least it's a nice meal for the mice!' she laughed.

Take one PICNIC CARD from your LUNCHBOX. Now go to 150.

306

Not only did they find a spare key but also a codebook! They were both lying under a rock exactly 30 metres from the barrel: just like the scrap of paper had said. But as they were about to put the key to the lock, they heard it being turned from the other side. Someone was releasing them! They wondered who on earth it could be . . .

If you don't already have it, put the CODEBOOK CARD into your RUCKSACK. Now go to 295.

307

'I wonder where that pot-hole was?' asked Dick, thinking they must have passed it somewhere. The very next moment, he had

disappeared! 'Dick, where are you?' they all shouted with anxiety. Then they saw the top of his head poking out from a large hole. If it hadn't been for his rucksack, he would have fallen right through! They grabbed hold of his arms, pulling him up. Although he was perfectly all right himself, he had dropped his lunchbox in the fall and spilt most of his sandwiches. They were much too dirty to pick up again.

Take one PICNIC CARD from your LUNCHBOX. Now go to 178.

308

The Five were part way up the steep, rocky path when they suddenly froze in their tracks. A light started to flash from above! 'It can't be!' exclaimed George in horror, 'it can't be The Wreckers' Tower, surely?' Then they noticed a small motor boat tossing on the waves below. The light seemed to be luring it into the rocks, just like all those years ago! They could barely watch as it came nearer and nearer to the cliffs but it somehow managed to steer right into the cove. Then something strange happened. Several men came running out of the passage to unload some packages from it. Just as the boat started to move out into the water again, the men made their way towards the bottom of the secret path. 'Quick, let's hurry!' said Julian, 'those men look up to no good.' They hadn't climbed much further when they noticed a hole half-hidden by a rock. 'Look, it's the entrance to a tunnel!' exclaimed Dick, peering inside. Seeing the men coming closer, they decided to crawl in.

Throw the FAMOUS FIVE DICE to decide who is to enter first.

JULIAN thrown	go to 208
DICK thrown	go to 176
GEORGE thrown	go to 259
ANNE thrown	go to 99
TIMMY thrown	go to 39
MYSTERY thrown	go to 122

309

Timmy led them, wagging his tail, to an old canal. The canal was covered with weed and looked as if it hadn't been used for ages! 'It was probably for carrying clay in the old days,' said Julian. 'There were lots of clay mines near here and water was an easy means of transporting it.' They followed the canal until it disappeared into a long tunnel. The path still ran alongside it inside but they weren't sure whether they should enter. Dick said it wouldn't be so bad with a torch and so they began to search for them in their rucksacks.

Use your TORCH CARD to light up the way by placing exactly over the shape below. If you don't have one in your RUCKSACK, go to 246 instead.

```
(/ GINH:,   ONMBHU  FR  ?MKJ:TIJHG  I OF
   AR  ? NO   !  ?&  U:,  BNJ?      UY!
   WMNBT     ?D!JM:LKFTG!  W I:LOU O
   FUNNY    INNI    T BGNFDH:M EI
```

They stopped for a talk only a few metres away. 'We'll hide the stuff at the north end of the pond,' said one of them in a gruff voice. The Five kept as quiet as they could, wondering how they were going to escape without being noticed. Anne suggested setting Timmy on to them but George whispered that they might have a gun. While they were thinking up other ideas, Julian decided to look up the pond on the map. It would be useful information to give to the police!

Use your MAP CARD to find out which square the pond is in — then follow the instruction. If you don't have one, you'll have to guess which instruction to follow.

If you think C2   go to 140

If you think B2   go to 228

If you think D2   go to 209

'Quick, let's get moving,' said Julian, 'I'm sure they can't be up to any good.' They hadn't climbed much further when they noticed a piece of material tied to a twig growing from the rock. Embroidered on the material was a message. *FOR SECRET TUNNEL* it began ... but the rest was in code. They quickly looked for a codebook before the men came any nearer.

Use your CODEBOOK CARD to decode the message — then follow the instruction. If you don't have one, go to 103 instead.

A few steps more and they had finally reached the top! 'What a wonderful view!' they all cried. But there wasn't time to admire the view for long. There was a tower to find! They were wondering which way to look when there was a sudden flash of light. 'Perhaps it's the tower!' exclaimed Julian, ' – but where did the flash come from?' They were hoping it would flash again so they could tell. But there was nothing. Then George had a great idea! They could use one of their torches to pretend it was a return signal. That might make the tower send out another flash. Then all they had to do was follow it!

*Use your **TORCH CARD** to try out George's idea by placing exactly over the shape below — then follow the instruction. If you don't have one, go to 223 instead.*

(/GINH:,   ONMBHU FR ?MKJ:TIJHG I OF
J   GHBT&G (JW,M JHG MO?MKJ
'N MKK   I BIFFO?!   UGFN   /NE B
MBHE YH ID !QAGASGJ H   HUTTH

THE ENID BLYTON TRUST
FOR CHILDREN

We hope you have enjoyed the adventures of the children in this book. Please think for a moment about those children who are too ill to do the exciting things you and your friends do.

Help them by sending a donation, large or small, to the ENID BLYTON TRUST FOR CHILDREN. The Trust will use all your gifts to help children who are sick or handicapped and need to be made happy and comfortable.

Please send your postal orders or cheques to:

The Enid Blyton Trust For Children,
Lee House,
London Wall,
London EC2Y 5AS.

Thank you very much for your help.